AF600646

A COMPARATIVE STUDY OF THE CHRISTIAN CONSTITUTION OF STATES AND THE CONSTITUTION OF THE PHILIPPINE COMMONWEALTH

The Catholic University of America
Canon Law Studies
No. 206

A Comparative Study of the Christian Constitution of States and the Constitution of the Philippine Commonwealth

BY

ALEXANDER AYSON OLALIA, S.T.L., J.C.L.
Priest of the Archdiocese of Manila, P. I.

A DISSERTATION

SUBMITTED TO THE FACULTY OF THE SCHOOL OF CANON LAW OF THE CATHOLIC UNIVERSITY OF AMERICA IN PARTIAL FULFILLMENT OF THE REQUIREMENTS FOR THE DEGREE OF DOCTOR OF CANON LAW

The Catholic University of America Press
Washington, D. C.
1944

NIHIL OBSTAT:

Eduardus G. Roelker, S.T.D., J.C.D.,
Censor Deputatus.

IMPRIMATUR:

✠ Geraldus P. O'Hara, D.D., J.U.D.,
Episcopus Savannensis-Atlantensis.

In urbe Savannah, Ga., 18 Julii, 1944.

Murray & Heister
Washington, D. C.

Printed by
Times and News Publishing Co.
Gettysburg, Pa., U. S. A.

FOREWORD

It is the purpose of this dissertation; first, to study the general principles of a Christian Constitution of States laid down by the teachings of the Church and repeatedly voiced by the Roman Pontiffs in their Encyclical Letters; secondly, to contrast with the said principles the Constitution of the Philippine Commonwealth.

In view of the increasing influence of subversive principles upon which statesmen tried in vain to base the whole structure of civil society, Leo XIII, solicitous for the general welfare of nations, had issued several instructions, grounded on the soundest principles of reason and revelation, about the Christian Constitution of States, Human Liberty, the Right Use of Political Power, and the Duties of Christian Citizens. In his Encyclical Letter "*Immortale Dei,*" the most comprehensive document in ecclesiastical public law, he pointed out the doctrine of the Church about the Christian organization of States and, in addition, he contrasted the modern theories on Constitutional law with the teachings of the Church.

It is precisely a very singular merit of the Encyclical Letters of Leo XIII on this subject that, although they were written almost half a century ago, they are the only remedy for the present needs of civil society.

Thus, in this dissertation there are considered the principles upon which to base the organization of a Christian nation and the mutual relations between this and the Church. The Philippine Constitution under consideration is that of the Commonwealth drafted by the Constitutional Convention of 1935. Only those provisions, however, which have some connection with religion and the Church are here studied and contrasted with the ecclesiastical public law.

The principal reason that moved the writer to undertake this study is the fact that in the near future the Philippines will be an independent nation. A nation is like a building which must be constructed upon solid ground, if it is to be expected to resist victoriously the challenge of time, and to attain its end, the general welfare of the people.

* * *

The author takes this opportunity to express his cordial gratitude to the Faculty of the School of Canon Law of The Catholic University of America for their assiduous and wise direction, and to all those who, through their generosity and encouragement, made possible the preparation of this dissertation.

TABLE OF CONTENTS

PART ONE

PRINCIPLES OF A CHRISTIAN CONSTITUTION

PART ONE

The Christian Constitution of States

CHAPTER I

General Notions

ARTICLE I. DEFINITION OF SOCIETY

It is not difficult, according to Leo XIII in his Encyclical Letter *"Immortale Dei,"* to determine the proper form and character of a State. Christian philosophy clearly teaches the principles governing its whole structure.

> Man's natural instinct moves him to live in civil society, for he cannot, if dwelling apart, provide himself with the necessary requirements of life, nor procure the means of developing his mental and moral faculties.[1]

Society is the "union of several persons for a common good attainable by the use of common means."[2] According to this definition, every society must have four elements, namely: members, union, means, and purpose.

a) Members. It must be composed of several persons, at least of two. Only intelligent beings can form societies, due to the fact that the members should be gifted with both intelligence and will; the first, in order to know the purpose pursued and understand the selection of the means necessary to attain it; the second, in order to cooperate willingly with the other members in the common struggle to realize the desired aspiration.[3]

b) Union. Not any kind of union constitutes the second element of society. It must be a moral and enduring union which derives from the union of the minds and wills of the members,

---

[1] Leo XIII, Encyclical, *"Immortale Dei"* (1885)—*ASS*, XVIII, 162. Translation from John J. Wynne, *The Great Encyclical Letters of Pope Leo XIII* (New York, Benziger Brothers, 1903), p. 108.

[2] Cavagnis, *Institutiones Iuris Publici Ecclesiastici* (2. ed., Romae: Typis Societatis Catholicae Instructivae, 1888), p. 27.

[3] Taparelli, *Droit Naturel* (Translated from Italian into French by M. l'abbé C. A Ozanam, Paris, 1863), lib. III, pp. 131-132.

and in virtue of this union, the members morally form one body, and their common efforts are considered as one. Moreover, from such union, there arise certain juridical relations, namely: 1) a strict obligation on the part of the members to direct all their actions towards the objective of the society; 2) the right on the part of the society to oblige all the members to a cooperative activity for the attainment of such purpose.[4]

c) Means. The third element of society is the possession of the necessary means. These must be available for all the members without any exception and, besides, they must be proportionate and adapted to the common good.[5]

d) Purpose. A society must have its purpose. This objective should be: 1) lawful, it must be in strict conformity to the dictates of reason; 2) common, it must be the concern of all the members and not only of some individuals; 3) finally, it must be concrete, certain, and definite.[6]

It is worth-while to notice that among the four elements of society, the element *purpose* is of the most importance especially in its juridical aspect. It specifies, as a matter of fact, not only the nature of the society but its juridical status as well. 1) The nature of a society is the nature of its purpose. A society, therefore, which has for its objective the material welfare of its members is obviously a material society.[7] 2) Also, upon the nature of the purpose depends the juridical status; that is, the system of organization of a society, its rights over its members and its rights in relation to other societies.

a) The system of organization depends upon the nature of its purpose; if the objective of a society is not necessary, if the members are free to pursue it or not, then the form of organization is optional. It will be what the members freely determine. If, on the contrary, the objective is necessary, and besides, can be attained only by the member's living in association with others, the

---

[4] Cappello, *Summa Iuris Publici Ecclesiastici* (4. ed., Romae: apud Aedes Universitatis Gregorianae, 1936), p. 38.

[5] Ottaviani, *Institutiones Iuris Publici Ecclesiastici* (2. ed., 2 vols., Romae: Typis Polyglottis Vaticanis, 1935-1936), I, 42.

[6] Ottaviani, *op. cit.*, I, 40-41.

[7] Ottaviani, *op. cit.*, I, 44-45.

system of organization is regulated either by a pre-existing law which imposes a definite form of organization or by a determination on the part of the authority of the society.[8] In both cases, however, it is the purpose of the society which decides the nature or character of its organization.

b) Its rights over its members are determined by the nature of its objective. The rights of the society to demand from the members the required means to attain its purpose are regulated by the necessary or unnecessary relation which exists between the means and the objective. If the means are necessary for the attainment of its aim, a correlative juridical relation arises between the members and the society in regard to the means, that is, the right on the part of the society to demand them and an obligation on the part of the members to cooperate. Consequently, the society does not have any right to claim the members' activity, if this is by no means necessary or conducive to its objective.[9]

c) Finally, it is the end of a society that determines its rights before other corporations. In case of conflict with other societies in the use of the common means, that society whose purpose excels in importance and nobility prevails over the rights of others.[10]

It is a question disputed among authors whether authority pertains to the essence of society or not. This controverted problem is based on the fact that without authority no society can exist. Although, for a society it is *"conditio sine qua non,"* as Leo XIII clearly declared saying, "No society can hold together unless someone be over all, directing all to strive earnestly for the common good,"[11] nevertheless, it cannot be claimed as an essentially constituent factor. The reason is this: authority is nothing else but the right to oblige the members of a society to strive for the common purpose; it presupposes, therefore, the pre-existence of membership in a formally and previously constituted society. It may be justly called, because of its extreme importance, a conservative element of society.

---

[8] Ottaviani, *op. cit.*, I, 45-46.

[9] Ottaviani, *op. cit.*, I, 46.

[10] Cavagnis, *op. cit.*, p. 104.

[11] Leo XIII, Encyclical, *"Immortale Dei"* (1885)—*ASS*, XVIII, 162. Translation from Wynne, *The Great Encyclical Letters of Pope Leo XIII*, pp. 108-109.

ARTICLE II. DIVISION OF SOCIETY

I) Societies are juridical and non-juridical, according as the bond of unity is or is not juridical. The bond of unity is juridical when the society is empowered to impose an obligation on the members for the sake of the common good, and these are bound strictly to obey *"ex justitia"* and moreover the society has the right to demand obedience through compulsion in case of stubbornness of the members.[12] In a non-juridical association the members are striving for a common good without any binding obligation to do so.

Juridical societies are subdivided into juridically perfect and juridically imperfect. The first is a society which has as its final purpose a good complete in its own sphere self-sufficient and independent.[13] The second lacks one or more of the qualifications stated above; that is, its purpose is not apt to satisfy fully all the needs of the members; it does not possess all the necessary means; and, finally, it does not enjoy complete self-sufficiency.

II) Societies are necessary and free, according as membership in the society is compulsory or not.[14] The necessary society has its origin from two sources; either from nature itself or from a positive disposition of the Creator, e.g., conjugal society comes from an inborn impulse of human nature; the Church is a society of divine-positive institution. Free or voluntary societies, on the other hand, are those whose nature and purposes are freely fixed by the members, e.g., literary associations. These may be well classified as optional.

III) Societies are organic and inorganic, according as the members are societies formally constituted before their admission to membership, or they are mere individuals.

IV) Societies are public and private, according as the purpose is the common good or not. The Church and the State are public societies, although the former has for its objective both the

---

[12] Cavagnis, *op. cit.*, p. 28.

[13] Ottaviani, *op. cit.*, I, 57.

[14] Le Buffe and Hayes, *Jurisprudence* (3. ed., Fordham University Press, New York, 1938), p. 228. Cappello, *op. cit.*, p. 42.

sanctification of the faithful in general and the personal sanctity of each member in particular.

V) Societies are similar and dissimilar, according as their aims are or are not of the same category. The Church and the State both intend the highest or supreme common good but in different categories; the first has under its care the spiritual, and the second the temporal. They are, therefore, dissimilar.

VI) Societies are subordinate and coordinate, according as they are dependent upon one another or entirely independent. A society may be subordinate to another for three reasons: a) if its end constitutes a part of the objective of another society; b) if its purpose serves as a medium to the objective of another; c) lastly, if its end is of inferior nature.

VII) Societies are religious and profane, according as they pursue a spiritual or a purely material and temporal common good.[15]

---

[15] Cappello, *Summa Iuris Publici Ecclesiastici,* pp. 43, 44.

CHAPTER II

Society "in specie"

Article I. Definition of Civil Society

The civil society is "the stable union of families and individuals, united under one supreme authority, and by several other juridical bonds, in a determined territory for the purpose of obtaining by common external means that full self-sufficiency and that free exercise of their rights by which the complete and perfect end in the natural order is attainable."[1] The following, therefore, are the constituent factors of the State: people, the bond of unity, the common purpose, and the common means.

I) People—the first element necessarily required to form a nation is the union of several men, and principally of several families. The family is the original nucleus of human society.[2]

II) Bond of unity—this is formed by the interplay of three factors: territory, sovereignty, and ethnology. a) Territory—geographical unity and exactness of the boundaries of a territory are of great importance for the national constitution of a State. The first provides a basis for national integrity, and the second expedites the exercise of the governmental jurisdiction. The Jews, notwithstanding their traditional unity of religion, language, customs, ideas, etc., do not form a nation of their own, because they do not possess a common land. b) Sovereignty—this is one of the essential characteristics of a society perfectly juridical, as the State is. This supreme right which consists in the moral power to impose obligations on the citizens through laws and to sanction disobedience to the laws, causes and strengthens the unity of a nation. c) Ethnology—the unity of origin, race, re-

---

[1] Ottaviani, *Institutiones Iuris Publici Ecclesiastici,* II, 2. Translation by the writer.

[2] Pius XI, Encyclical, "*Ubi Arcano Dei*" (December 23, 1922)—*AAS,* XIV, p. 678.

ligion, language, traditions, customs, etc., helps to build up national unity.[3]

III) Purpose—this, as the definition itself states, must be good, complete and perfect in the temporal order. It is complete and perfect, if it satisfies the temporal needs of men who, if living apart, cannot permanently and efficiently provide them.

IV) Means—these must be common and, at the same time proportionate to the end pursued which is undoubtedly material and temporal, i.e., social and temporal prosperity.[4]

ARTICLE II. ORIGIN AND NATURE OF CIVIL SOCIETY

The civil society draws its origin from the fact that man is by nature sociable. Sociability is the natural instinct of man that moves him to live in society. Of course, he is not impelled physically to enter society for he really enjoys physical liberty to refrain from membership therein; he is, however, forced emotionally, i.e., by the reason of his natural inclinations and needs which normally cannot be satisfied outside the civil society. His natural inclination constrains him to seek the company of his fellow-men; he instinctively abhors solitude. He feels in his heart the necessity to communicate his sentiments and the generosity to participate in the good or evil fortune of others of his own kind.[5]

The exigencies of his corporal and spiritual life impel him to associate with many, as Leo XIII wisely teaches, "He [man] cannot, if dwelling apart, provide himself with the necessary requirements of life, nor procure the means of developing his mental and moral faculties. Hence, it is divinely ordained that he should lead his life—be it family, social, or civil—with his fellow-men, amongst whom alone his several wants can adequately be supplied."[6]

Some authors who, in their futile efforts to darken the clarity of the doctrine of the Church concerning the real origin of the

---

[3] Ottaviani, *op. cit.*, II, 3-6.

[4] Cappello, *Summa Iuris Publici Ecclesiastici*, p. 271.

[5] Le Buffe and Hayes, *op. cit.*, p. 231.

[6] Leo XIII, Encyclical, *"Immortale Dei"* (1885)—*ASS*, XVIII, 162. Translation from Wynne, *op. cit.*, p. 108.

civil society, had excogitated in different ages several systems entirely grounded upon arbitrary and atheistic principles. The two authors, who are worthy of consideration, because of their historical importance, are Hobbes and Rousseau.

Hobbes (1588-1679) asserted that man naturally endowed with a warlike spirit lived at first in continuous war with his fellow-men; was completely inept for society, and instinctively abhorred any kind of association with others.[7] Afterwards, men, tired of this hostile and intolerable condition, were forced to enter society in which they freely ceded all their individual rights to one who had to preside over them for the purpose of social peace and common defense.[8]

Rousseau (1712-1778) maintained, too, that man is by nature anti-social. His doctrine, however, differs partly from that of Hobbes, for according to Rousseau man was in the very beginning completely happy, virtuous, sufficient to himself, and essentially perfectible.[9] This innate desire for further perfection led men to display their good qualities in industries, in works of art, and in other enterprises, and this fact after a while caused countless rivalries, quarrels, and enmities among themselves. This state of things which made life intolerable for men induced them to form the civil society. "To do so without loss of personal freedom, there was but one way, namely, that all members should agree to merge all their rights, wills and personalities in one moral person and will, leaving the subject-members the satisfaction that he was obeying his own will thus merged, and so in possession still of full liberty in every act."[10]

ARTICLE III. END OF CIVIL SOCIETY

The purpose of the civil society is the common good of the citizens in the temporal order attainable not solely through the conservation of their lives, but also through the full development

[7] Hobbes, *Elementaria Philosophia de Cive* (*Amstelodami,* 1696), c. I, n. 12.
[8] Hobbes, *op. cit.,* c. VI, n. 16.
[9] Rousseau, *Du Contrat Social* (Paris, 1793), lib. I, c. I.
[10] Macksey, *The Catholic Encyclopedia,* Vol. XIV, p. 77, col., 2.

of their mental and moral faculties. The fulfillment of this obligation imposes on the part of the State the strict duty of securing the citizens in their right to life, liberty, and of affording them the opportunities socially necessary for the pursuit of temporal happiness.[11]

"In the plan of the Creator, society is a natural means which man can and must use to reach his destined end. Society is for man and not vice versa. This must not be understood in the sense of liberalistic individualism, which subordinates society to the selfish use of the individual; but only in the sense that by means of an organic union with society and by mutual collaboration the attainment of earthly happiness is placed within the reach of all. It is society which affords the opportunities for the development of all the individual and social gifts bestowed on human nature."[12] It must, therefore, take special care in the creation of all those measures and material conditions of life without which an orderly society can not exist.

Leo XIII clearly pointed out the end of the State saying: "The foremost duty, therefore, of the rulers of the State should be to make sure that the laws and institutions, the general character and administration of the commonwealth, shall be such as of themselves to realize public well-being and private prosperity."[13] The State, besides, must see to it that in the pursuit of the temporal welfare nothing impede the attainment of the eternal end of man. The Creator placed him in society not exclusively for his temporal happiness, but also and principally for his eternal destiny. "Hence civil society established for the common welfare, should not only safeguard the well-being of the community, but have also at heart the interest of its individual members, in such mode as not in any way to hinder, but in every manner to render as easy as may be, the possession of that high-

[11] Farges et Barbedette, *Philosophia Scholastica* (55. ed., 2 vols., Parisiis: Apud Berche et Pagis, Editores, 1932), II, 488, 489.

[12] Pius XI, Encyclical, *Divini Redemptoris*" (1937)—*AAS*, XXIX, 79. Translation from Koenig, *The Principles for Peace* (National Catholic Welfare Conference, Washington, D. C., 1943), n. 1222.

[13] Leo XIII, Encyclical, "*Rerum Novarum*" (1891)—*ASS*, XXIII, 656. Translation from Wynne, *op. cit.*, p. 227.

est and unchangeable good for which all should seek. Wherefore, for this purpose, care must specially be taken to preserve unharmed and unimpeded the religion whereof the practice is the link connecting man with God."[14]

It is evident, therefore, from the doctrine of Christian philosophy, that the State is by no means an end in itself; not something distinct from and superior to the citizens composing it, as some Philosophers, and, in our days, the Totalitarian Systems strongly advocate. The State is for the people a means to reach not only their temporal goal, but their ultimate destiny as well.

[14] Leo XIII, Encyclical, *"Immortale Dei"* (1885)—*ASS,* XVIII, 164. Translation from Wynne, *op. cit.,* p. III.

CHAPTER III

Civil Sovereignty

ARTICLE I. NOTION OF CIVIL SOVEREIGNTY

> But as no society can hold together unless some one be over all, directing all to strive earnestly for the common good; every civilized community must have a ruling authority, and this authority, no less than society itself, has its source in nature and has, consequently, God for its author. . . . The right to rule is not necessarily, however, bound up with any special mode of government.[1]

By civil sovereignty the author intends to signify in this article the supreme power in a nation. Sovereignty is the "right of the supreme civil ruler to direct effectively the subjects of a State to promote, by the cooperative efforts of their external action, social peace and temporal prosperity."[2] This supreme power is a moral faculty and not the mere sum of the physical might of the people focused in a common centre of force called the authority, as some Materialists asserted.[3] Hence it does not bind merely the physical actions of the subjects, for within its proper sphere it imposes upon their consciences the strict obligation of obedience. It is called supreme, because it is completely independent in the natural order, save in things contrary to natural law. Finally, it directs effectively the subjects towards the common end through laws and sanctions.

---

[1] Leo XIII, Encyclical, *"Immortale Dei"* (1885)—*ASS*, XVIII, 162. Translation from Wynne, *op. cit.*, pp. 108, 109.

[2] Le Buffe and Hayes, *op. cit.*, p. 229.

[3] Pius IX, *"Syllabus,"* prop. 60. cf. Denzinger-Bannwart, *Enchiridion Symbolorum, Definitionum et Declarationum de Rebus Fidei et Morum* (18-20. ed., Friburgi, Brisgoviae: Herder & Co., Typographi Editores Pontificii, 1932), n. 1760.

ARTICLE II. ORIGIN OF CIVIL SOVEREIGNTY

Leo XIII clearly enunciates the natural origin of the civil sovereignty in this term. "This authority, no less than society itself, has its source in nature" [and since God is the author of nature, there naturally follows from this the conclusion that God is the fountain of all civil authority]. "There is no power but from God."[4]

In conformity with one's knowledge on the origin of sovereignty will vary one's respect for and submission to that same authority. Civil obedience is grounded thereon; patriotism and loyalty are conditioned thereby. "Then truly will the majesty of the law meet with the dutiful and willing homage of the people, when they are convinced that their rulers hold authority from God, and feel that it is a matter of justice and duty to obey them, and to show them reverence and fealty, united to a love not unlike that which children show their parents."[5]

ARTICLE III. NECESSITY OF CIVIL AUTHORITY

The natural example of the human body which cannot continue in existence without a head gives us the proper idea as to how indispensable is authority in a society. Since the State is similar to a human body, for like the body it is composed of several members, i.e., officials and classes of people, far less easily, therefore, could it be conserved one and efficient without some one who governs it and who is responsible for the attainment of the common good.[6]

Besides, since there are many ways that lead to the final aim of the civil society, a diversity of viewpoints and judgments naturally arises among the citizens. There must necessarily be, therefore, some one who can with supreme authority decide which of the many courses is to be followed by all the members in pursuing

---

[4] Rom. XIII, 1.

[5] Leo XIII, Encyclical, *"Immortale Dei"* (1885)—*ASS,* XVIII, 163. Translation from Wynne, *op. cit.,* p. 110.

[6] Cathrein, *Philosophia Moralis in Usum Scholarum* (6. ed., 1907, Friburgi Brisgoviae, Herder: Typographi Editoris Pontificii), pp. 364, 365.

the common good.[7] To this effect St. Thomas says: "Now a social life cannot exist among a number of people unless under the presidency of one to look after the common good; for many, as such, seek many things, whereas one attends to one. Wherefore the Philosopher (Aristotle) says, in the beginning of the *Politics,* that whenever many things are adjusted to one thing, we shall always find one at the head directing them."[8]

The same doctrine is taught by St. Bellarmine. "Now, truly, if human nature needs social life, certainly it also needs a rule and ruler, for it is impossible for a multitude to hold together for any length of time unless there be one who governs it, and who is responsible for the common welfare; just as, if there were not in each one of us a soul to govern and unite the parts and powers and conflicting elements of which we are made, immediately all would disintegrate. Hence it is written, 'Where there is no governor, the people shall fall.' Finally, society is order among many, for a disorderly and scattered multitude is not called society; moreover, what is order than a certain succession of inferiors and superiors? Therefore, rulers have been necessarily ordained, if society is to endure."[9]

ARTICLE IV. LEGISLATIVE POWER

By means of government authority directs the subjects of the State towards their temporal prosperity. The government, as the organ of the supreme power in a nation, has a threefold function, namely: legislative, judicial, and coercive.

Legislative power is the right to impose, in an obligatory form, that which is necessary for the attainment of the common good.[10] The State, as perfect society, is duly entitled to this right. It can,

---

[7] Cathrein, *ibid.,* p. 365.

[8] St. Thomas, *Summa Theologica,* I, q. 96, art. 4. A translation by the Fathers of the English Dominican Province (8 vols., New York: Benziger Brothers, 1913-1937).

[9] St. Bellarmine, *De Laicis or The Treatise on Civil Government,* translated by Murphy, K. E. (New York: Fordham University Press, 1928), p. 22.

[10] Cappello, *Summa Iuris Publici Ecclesiastici,* p. 72.

therefore, demand from the citizens not only that which is immediately necessary for achieving the temporal prosperity of the nation in general, but also that which is in some way conducive to that end. The State determines and prescribes these means publicly through its legislation. Thus a law is "a rule prescribed by the sovereign of society to his subjects, either in order to lay an obligation upon them of doing or omitting certain things, under the commination of punishment; or to leave them at liberty to act or not in other things just as they think proper, and to secure to them, in this respect, the full enjoyment of their rights."[11]

ARTICLE V. JUDICIAL POWER

In judicial power is centered the right of the civil society to interpret authentically the true sense of its laws, and to judge whether the citizens direct their common effort for the common good in conformity with the laws or not.[12] This power is an indispensable complement of the legislative power of the State, inasmuch as it gives the authentic interpretation of the laws and properly executes the application thereof to particular cases. Thus, the State has the right to settle controversies arising between the citizens themselves, or between the State and her subjects.

Moreover, the State must have the judicial power, because it is necessary for the attainment of the general welfare of the people. It is not enough that the means to achieve the common good are clearly prescribed by the laws, but it is absolutely necessary that someone see to it that the laws are exactly obeyed and that the means are properly applied.

ARTICLE VI. COERCIVE POWER

In its coercive power is seated the right of the State to demand obedience through compulsion, if necessary, and to inflict

---

[11] Burlamaqui, *The Principle of Natural and Political Law* (5. ed., 2 vols., translated into English by Nugent, Cambridge: The University Press, 1776), II, 65.

[12] Cappello, *op. cit.*, p. 76.

temporal penalties upon the subjects convicted by the law.[13] The necessity of this power in a civil society is evident. The legislative and the judicial powers would be futile, if the State could not exercise the right to punish. Since there are many in every community who through malice undermine the national safety and thereby frustrate the purpose of the civil society, it is necessary that the government should have the power to punish such citizens and to force them to submission. And this is done by the coercive power of the State.

ARTICLE VII. THE FORM OF GOVERNMENT IN CIVIL SOCIETY

If we consider authority not in itself, but in relation to the person, or subject who holds and exercises it, authority can take several forms, according as it is in the hands of one, or is exercised by a selected group of persons, or by the people themselves through representation. Hence, we have the three simple forms of government: Monarchy, Aristocracy, and Democracy, to which Tyranny, Oligarchy, and Anarchy are opposed respectively as the abuses thereof.

Although the Supreme Legislator has decreed from all eternity that man should live in society and that there should be presiding authority therein, he has not, however, determined the way to exercise this power to rule. It follows from this that, by the will of the Creator, the people are empowered to decide for themselves the regime of government which is more or less adapted to their customs and traditions.[14]

The Church has never prohibited the people from selecting this or that system of government, provided religion and morality are safeguarded.[15] Any of the three, Monarchy, Aristocracy, or Democracy, is legitimate and good although none of the three forms

---

[13] Cappello, *op. cit.,* p. 79. Compulsion is the act by which one is constrained to do against his will something which otherwise he would not have done.

[14] Leo XIII, Encyclical, *"Au Milieu des Sollicitudes"* (Feb. 16, 1892)—*ASS,* XXIV, 523.

[15] Ottaviani, *Institutiones Iuris Publici Ecclesiastici,* II, 34.

is entirely perfect.[16] For this reason Leo XIII speaking about the various political governments that succeeded one another in France states: "The Empire, the Monarchy, and the Republic . . . in all truth it may be affirmed that each of them is good, provided it lead straight to its end—that is to say, to the common good for which social authority is constituted. . . . In this order of speculative ideas, Catholics, like all other citizens, are free to prefer one form of government to another precisely because no one of these social forms is, in itself, opposed to the principles of sound reason nor to the maxims of Christian doctrine. . . ."[17]

No definite answer can be given to the question: Which is the best form of government for a nation? In order that a system of government may be justly admitted as the best for a certain nation, it is not enough that it be perfect and excellent in form, but also, and above all, it must be adapted to the character and customs of the people, and, finally, the legislation should be entirely animated by Christian principles, for, as has already happened many times, "under a system of government most excellent in form, legislation could be detestable; while quite the opposite, under a regime most imperfect in form might be found excellent legislation."[18]

In general it would be safe to state with Brosnahan that "the best form of government is that which is suited to the political capacity and character of the people as determined by historical causes, and in which authority is so exercised and liberty so secured as to inspire citizens with loyalty. For the political temperament of modern people, at least, this is best effected in a constitutional and representative government, in which the functions of government are distributed in different departments, but in such a way as to preserve organic unity."[19]

St. Thomas who lived in the thirteenth century makes this remarkable assertation: "The best form of government is in a

---

[16] Brosnahan, *Prolegomena to Ethics with a Digest of Ethics* (edited by Le Buffe, New York, 1941), p. 319.

[17] Leo XIII, Encyclical, *"Au Milieu des Sollicitudes"* (Feb. 16, 1892)—*ibid.* Translation from Wynne, *op. cit.*, p. 255.

[18] Leo XIII, *ibid.*, pp. 525, 526. Translation from Wynne, *loc. cit.*, pp. 258, 259.

[19] Brosnahan, *ibid.*

State or Kingdom, wherein one is given the power to preside over all; while under him are others having governing powers; and yet a government of this kind is shared by all, both because all are eligible to govern, and because the rulers are chosen by all. For this is the best form of polity; being partly kingdom, since there is one at the head of all; partly aristocracy, insofar as a number of persons are set in authority; partly democracy, i.e., government by the people, insofar as the rulers can be chosen from the people, and the people have the right to choose their rulers."[20]

ARTICLE VIII. THE SUBJECT OF CIVIL AUTHORITY

From the fact that authority comes from God we cannot logically conclude that the rulers are also of divine institution. The passage of the Holy Scripture, "There is no power but from God,"[21] proves merely the origin of authority considered as such. God does not give the power directly and immediately to the rulers of nations, e.g., Kings or Presidents. No man, as a matter of fact, has been delegated expressly and by divine revelation to rule over the people, except in the case of the Jewish nation of centuries ago.

The fact that authority is exercised in this or in that form, held by one or more persons, depends upon the free consent of the people. This free consent can be manifested in various ways; the most common and ordinary mode is by election.[22]

So far we have studied, first, that authority in itself derives from God, and, secondly, that it is within the power of the people to select according to their customs and traditions the form of government and the ruler they consider best. The latter part of this doctrine has been widely misunderstood in our days. It has attributed to the people an absolute power without any reference to God, thus the theory of those who advocate that all authority is conferred upon the ruler, selected to govern the nation, either

[20] St. Thomas, *Summa Theologica*, I-II, q. 105, art 1.

[21] Rom. XIII, 1.

[22] Ottaviani, *Institutiones Iuris Publici Ecclesiastici*, II, 26.

directly by the people and indirectly by God or directly by God Himself. On both sides of the controversy there are weighty authors. St. Bellarmine;[23] Suarez;[24] and other scholastics maintain that the ruler, King or President, receives the power to govern directly from the people. One of the principal arguments upon which they base their position is the following: supreme authority in a State is of divine institution. No ruler, however, possesses this authority *"ex iure"* in a nation. Therefore, they conclude, the power must derive from the people themselves.

The major and the minor are evident. The conclusion is by no means cogent, for it does not follow from the premises stated. It would be perfectly sufficient for the constitution of the State, if the people elect the ruler and once selected God gives immediately the power to rule. It is in no way necessary that the people should delegate authority to the ruler directly and immediately.

This doctrine, which teaches the general principle that all power comes from God, and advocates as a probable opinion that God communicate directly the supreme power to the multitude who in turn are obliged to transfer it to the selected ruler, must not be confounded with that theory condemned by the Church.

The opposite opinion asserts that God is the one who directly and immediately confers the power. The defenders of this theory, Jacques Benigne Bossuet (1627-1704)[25] among them, state as follows: that by which the multitude are united in society exists before and independently of the people. As a matter of fact, authority is that by which the multitude are united in society. Therefore, they conclude, authority is not in the multitude, and as a consequence, they do not confer power upon the ruler.

Since the Church has not decided definitively the question, Catholics can adhere to either side of the controversy; the second opinion, however, seems to enjoy in a greater degree conformity

---

[23] *De Laicis,* lib. III, c. VI—Murphy, pp. 10, 12.

[24] *Defensio Fidei Catholicae* (*Opera Omnia,* ed. nova, a Carolo Berton, 26 vols., Parisiis: Apud Ludovicum Vives, Bibliopolam Editorem, 1859), XXIV, lib. III, c. II, 10, 12.

[25] *Controverse, Œuvres Complètes,* XXXIX-XL, *Defensio Declarationis Cleri Gallicani* (Paris, 1878), lib. I, sect. I, c. III, pp. 269, 272.

with the doctrine of the Church. Leo XIII says: "But it is of importance to remark in this place that those who may be placed over the State may in certain cases be chosen by the will and decision of the multitude, without opposing or impugning the Catholic doctrine. And by this choice; in truth, the prince is designated, but the rights of princedom are not thereby conferred: nor is the authority delegated to him, but the person by whom it is to be exercised is determined upon."[26]

Leo XIII also says: "The sovereignty of the people, however, and this without any reference to God, is held to reside in the multitude; which is doubtless a doctrine exceedingly well calculated to flatter and to inflame many passions, but which lacks all reasonable proof, and all power of insuring public safety and preserving order. Indeed from the prevalence of this teaching, things have come to such a pass that many hold as an axiom of civil jurisprudence that seditions may be rightly fostered. For the opinion prevails that princes are nothing more than delegates chosen to carry out the will of the people; whence it necessarily follows that all things are as changeable as the will of the people, so that risk of public disturbance is ever hanging over our heads."[27]

---

[26] Leo XIII, Encyclical, *"Diuturnum"* (June 29, 1881)—*ASS*, XIV, 4. Translation from *The Tablet* (London, July 16, 1881), p. 109.

[27] Leo XIII, Encyclical, *"Immortale Dei"* (1885)—*ASS*, XVIII, 171, 172. Translation from Wynne, *The Great Encyclical Letters of Pope Leo XIII*, p. 123.

CHAPTER IV

Nature of Civil Society

ARTICLE I. THE STATE IS A PUBLIC AND JURIDICAL SOCIETY

a) The State is a public society. A public society is that which pursues the common good of the members as its main objective. The civil society, as a matter of fact, has for its main objective the general prosperity of the nation as a whole. For this reason, the State is truly a public society.

b) The State is a juridical society. A juridical society is that which is empowered to impose on the members obligations which, for the sake of achieving the common end, bind in conscience so that the members are strictly bound by justice to obey. The State is a society of this kind, because it directs authoritatively the common efforts of all the members towards the common good and has the power to coerce those who deny their cooperation.

This juridical constitution of the civil society is not a human institution, but proceeds from nature itself. "Hence it is divinely ordained that he [man] should lead his life—be it family, social, or civil—with his fellow-men, among whom alone his several wants can be adequately satisfied. But as no society can hold together unless some one be over all, directing all to strive earnestly for the common good; every civilized community must have a ruling authority, and this authority, no less than society itself, has its source in nature, and has, consequently, God for its author."[1]

More definitely Pius XI says: "Man cannot be exempted from his divinely-imposed obligations towards civil society, and the representatives of authority have the right to coerce him when he refuses without reason to do his duty."[2]

---

[1] Leo XIII, Encyclical, *"Immortale Dei"* (1885)—*ASS,* XVIII, 162. Translation from Wynne, *loc. cit.,* pp. 108, 109.

[2] Pius XI, Encyclical, *"Divini Redemptoris"* (March 19, 1937)—*ASS,* XXIX, 79. Translation from Koenig, *Principles for Peace,* n. 1223.

ARTICLE II. THE STATE IS A SOCIETY JURIDICALLY PERFECT

A juridically perfect society is that which has as its purpose some good, complete in its own sphere, as well as all the means necessary for achieving that end, and is in its own order self-sufficient and independent. The essential reasons, therefore, for the juridical perfection of a society are the pursuance of a purpose which satisfies all the needs of the members, the possession of all the necessary means to attain its end, and, consequently, self-sufficiency and independence. But the State has for its purpose a good which is complete in its own sphere and also possesses all the means to attain its objective. Hence, the State is juridically perfect.

The Church openly acknowledges the juridical perfection of the State in the temporal order. "The Almighty, therefore, has given the charge of the human race to two powers, the ecclesiastical and the civil, the one being set over divine and the other over human things. Each in its kind is supreme, each has fixed limits within which it is contained, limits which are defined by the nature and special object of the province of each, so that there is, we may say, an orbit traced out within which the action of each is brought into play by its own natural right. . . ."[3]

ARTICLE III. THE STATE IS A LEGAL PERSON

Besides physical persons there are the artificial ones called legal persons. A legal person although void of physical entity and unity enjoys all the privileges and rights of a natural person. It is inviolable in its rights, and is independent and distinct from all other persons either natural and artificial.[4] This legal person may be defined as a juridical being, considered as self-subsistent, to which is attributed the right to exist and to dispose of itself freely as a person *"sui iuris."*[5]

---

[3] Leo XIII, Encyclical, *"Immortale Dei"* (November 1, 1885)—*ASS*, XVIII, 166. Translation from Wynne, *op. cit.*, p. 114.

[4] Vermeersch-Creusen, *Epitome Iuris Canonici* (3 vols.; vol. I, 6. ed., 1937; vol. II, 5. ed., 1934; vol. III, 5. ed., 1936; Mechliniae et Romae, Dessain), I, n. 222.

[5] Ottaviani, *Institutiones Iuris Publici Ecclesiastici*, I, n. 27.

The State is by nature constituted a moral or legal person, gifted with inviolable rights to existence and to attain its purpose. That it is moral entity clearly appears from its definition. The State has been established and ordained by God to attain the general welfare of the human race; "*ipso facto*" and "*iure naturali*" it is given the inviolable right to possess all the means necessary to that end. Therefore, the civil society "*iure naturali*" is a legal person, an inviolable subject of rights, independent and distinct from all other natural and artificial persons.

SUMMARY

Summarizing all that has been said about the civil society regarding its whole social and juridical structure, it is to be stated that the State is a true society with all the constituent factors thereof; it is a natural society, because its origin derives from nature itself; it is necessary, because without it the temporal happiness of men is unattainable; it is public, because it promotes the general welfare of the people as a nation, and not as individuals; it is juridical, because it is empowered to coerce its members to the fulfillment of their duties; it is juridically perfect, because it pursues as its final end a good complete in its own sphere, and possesses all the means necessary to that end; as a consequence of its juridical perfection the State is self-sufficient and independent; it has its own proper government invested with supreme authority in the natural order; and finally, the State is a legal person, because it enjoys all the rights and privileges attributed to a natural person.

CHAPTER V

The Church as a Society

ARTICLE I. DEFINITION OF THE CHURCH AS A SOCIETY

> For the only-begotten Son of God established on earth a society which is called the Church. . . . This society is made up of men, just as civil society is, and yet is supernatural and spiritual, on account of the end for which it was founded, and of the means by which it aims at attaining that end . . . it is a society chartered as of right divine, perfect in its nature and in its title, to possess in itself and by itself . . . needful provision for its maintenance and action.[1]

The Church is the congregation of all the faithful, who, being baptized, profess the same doctrine, partake of the same sacraments, and are governed by lawful pastors under one visible head, the Pope.[2] This definition contains all the constituent factors of a true society. a) Members—The faithful all over the world form the membership of the Church. b) Bond of unity—The unity of faith and government preserves the Church one and entire. c) Means—The Sacraments are the channels by which the members receive all that they need in the supernatural sphere to attain their eternal destiny. d) Purpose—The Church "has for her immediate and natural purpose the saving of souls and securing our happiness in heaven. Yet in regard to things temporal she is the source of benefits as manifold and great as if the chief end of her existence were to ensure the prospering of our earthly life."[3]

That the Church is a society is a fact that cannot be denied;

[1] Leo XIII, Encyclical, "*Immortale Dei*" (November 1, 1885)—*ASS*, XVIII, 164, 165. Translation from Wynne, *op. cit.*, p. 112.

[2] Cappello, *Summa Iuris Publici Ecclesiastici*, pp. 109, 110.

[3] Leo XIII, Encyclical, "*Immortale Dei*" (November 1, 1885)—*ASS*, XVIII, 163. Translation from Wynne, *op. cit.*, p. 107.

it is a truth evident to everybody. In all nations she has members who obey her commandments, partake of her sacraments through which her Divine Founder communicates his sanctifying grace and friendship.

ARTICLE II. DIVINE ORIGIN OF THE CHURCH

It is not difficult to prove from Holy Scripture that Jesus Christ while on earth established a society called the Church. Our Lord Himself directly and immediately founded the Church with all the constituent elements of a true society: members, bond of unity, purpose, and means.

a) Members—The Holy Gospels testify that several men followed Jesus Christ and became his disciples; and from these he chose twelve (whom he also named apostles).[4]

"And going up a mountain he called to him men of his own choosing, and they came to him. And he appointed twelve that they might be with him and that he send them forth to preach. . . ."[5]

He gave to the twelve Apostles the power to preach the Gospel to all nations and peoples that they may believe in him and be members of the Church outside of which there is no salvation. "All power in heaven and on earth has been given to me. Go, therefore, and make disciples of all nations, baptizing them in the name of the Father, and of the Son, and of the Holy Spirit, teaching them to observe all that I have commanded you; and behold, I am with you all days, even unto the consummation of the world."[6]

b) Purpose—The common end pursued in this society could not be other than the salvation of souls; for this reason the Father had sent his only-begotten Son to this world. Thus Our Lord says: "But now set free from sin and become slaves to God, you have your fruit unto sanctification, and as your end, life everlasting."[7]

---

[4] St. Luke, VI, 13.

[5] St. Mark, III, 13-14.

[6] St. Matth., XXVIII, 19, 20.

[7] Rom., VI, 22.

"For God so loved the world that he gave his only-begotten Son, that those who believe in him may not perish, but may have life everlasting. For God did not send his Son into the world in order to judge the world, but that the world be saved through him."[8]

c) Means—The sacraments of the New Law were instituted by our Lord as the principal means for men's salvation,[9] and these sacraments are neither more nor less than seven in number, namely: Baptism, Confirmation, Penance, Holy Eucharist, Extreme Unction, Holy Order, and Matrimony.[10] Their respective institution is recorded in the Holy Scripture.[11] The Church, in virtue of the divine power given her by Jesus Christ, has instituted the sacramentals as other means to obtain the common end. "Sacramentals are sacred objects and actions which the Church, in a certain imitation of the sacraments, employs for the purpose of obtaining especially spiritual favor through her intercession."[12] Moreover, in virtue of her mission to lead her members to heaven, she has the right to possess temples and other sacred places necessary for divine worship.[13] That she is entitled also to possess temporal goods which are conducive to her purpose is clearly stated in the following canons:

"The Catholic Church and the Apostolic See have an inherent right freely and independently of the civil power to acquire, keep and administer temporal goods for the prosecution of the proper purposes of the Church."[14] "The Church has, moreover, the right independently of the civil power to demand from the faithful the necessary means for conducting divine worship, for

---

[8] St. John, III, 16, 17.

[9] Cf. Canon 731, § 1.

[10] Conc. Trident., sess., VII, *de sacramentis in genere,* c. I: cf. Denzinger-Bannwart, n. 844.

[11] St. Matth., XXVIII, 19; St. John, XVI, 7, 8; St. Matth., XXVI, 26, 28; St. John, XX, 22, 23; St. James, V, 14, 15; I Timothy, V, 14; Ephesians, V, 31.

[12] Canon 1144. Translation from Woywod, *A Practical Commentary on the Code of Canon Law* (5. ed., 2 vols., New York: Jos. F. Wagner, 1939), I, n. 1187.

[13] Ottaviani, *Institutiones Iuris Publici Ecclesiastici,* I, 175.

[14] Canon 1495. Translation from Woywood, *op. cit.,* II, n. 1487.

the decent maintenance of the clergy and other ministers, and her other proper purposes."[15] "The Church can acquire temporal goods by all just means which are sanctioned in the case of others by the natural or the positive law."[16]

This right claimed by the Church to possess even temporal goods necessary for the attainment of her purpose is a logical sequence which follows from her divine institution as a society established by Christ. If the Founder gave to the Church the duty to govern and guide men in the spiritual order, it is logical that Christ has given her also all the rights and powers incident to her mission. Leo XIII referring to the temporal dominion which the Holy See exercises in the Papal States says: "And assuredly all ought to hold that it was not without a singular disposition of God's providence that this power of the Church was provided with civil sovereignty as the surest safeguard of her independence."[17]

d) Bond of unity—Besides the unity of faith, Jesus Christ set over all the faithful one supreme authority for the purpose of safeguarding the purity of the doctrine he taught while on earth, and of governing the members in their pilgrimage towards the eternal destiny. He promised this supreme power to Peter saying, "And I say to thee, thou art Peter and upon this rock I shall build my Church. . . . And I will give thee the keys of the Kingdom of heaven; and whatever thou shalt bind on earth shall be loosed in heaven."[18] "Feed my lambs . . . ," "Feed my sheep . . . ,"[19] were the words by which the invisible head of the Church conferred the supreme authority upon the first Vicar, his visible successor on earth.

This is, therefore, the divine origin of the Church with all its essential elements directly and expressly instituted by Christ Who purposely established the Church as a true and visible society on earth. "She [the Church] is not an association of Christians

---

[15] Canon 1496. Translation from Woywood, *ibid.*

[16] Canon 1499. Translation from Woywood, *op. cit.*, II, n. 1489.

[17] Leo XIII, Encyclical, *"Immortale Dei"* (November 1, 1885)—*ASS*, XVIII, 166. Translation from Wynne, *op. cit.*, p. 114.

[18] St. Matth., XVI, 18-19.

[19] St. John, XXI, 15-17.

brought together by chance, but is a divinely established and admirably constituted society, having for its direct and proximate purpose to lead the world to peace and holiness. And since the Church alone has, through the grace of God, received the means necessary to realize such end, she has her fixed laws, special spheres of action, and a certain method, fixed and conformable to her nature, of governing Christian people."[20]

Against this doctrine the Protestants, Modernists and Liberals affirm that Christ did not intend to establish a society; the present social form of the Church was not conceived and planned by Christ, but derives from the natural and social instinct of men to live always in society.

---

[20] Leo XIII, Encyclical, "*Sapientiae Christianae*" (January 10, 1890), cf. *Codicis Iuris Canonici Fontes cura Emi. Petro Card. Gasparri editi*, 9 vols., Romae (Civitate Vaticana): Typis Polyglottis Vaticanis, 1923-1939 (Vols., VII-IX ed. cura et studio Emi. Justiniani Card. Serèdi.), n. 605. Translation from Wynne, *op. cit.*, p. 195.

CHAPTER VI

Nature of the Church

ARTICLE I. THE CHURCH IS A PUBLIC SOCIETY

A society is called public which, for its institution, organization and destination, pursues an end capable of satisfying the social, external and general needs of the public.[1] The Church is a public society because of her institution, her universality, and her activity. a) Because of her institution—the Church has been established that by her all men may be led to eternal salvation. b) Because of her universality—the Church was founded by Christ for all times and for all nations, and is, according to the promise of Christ and of the prophets, to be spread over the whole world.[2] c) Because of her activity—the benefits which the Church confers on the civil society are unparalleled in excellence and in effectiveness in fostering the spiritual and temporal prosperity of the public in general.

"The Church does not separate a proper regard for temporal welfare from solicitude for the eternal. If she subordinates the former to the latter according to the words of her divine Founder, 'Seek ye first the kingdom of God and His justice, and all these things shall be added unto you,' she is nevertheless so far from being unconcerned with human affairs, so far from hindering civil progress and material advancement, that she actually fosters and promotes them in the most sensible and efficacious manner."[3]

"It is proper and it is certainly involved in the duty of the Holy See that We should foster and strenuously promote all those things whence men, both individually and in their social life as citizens, can draw help for the alleviation of those many ills which, like the fruits of a diseased tree, have followed upon

---

[1] Ottaviani, *op. cit.*, II, 178.

[2] Matth., XXVIII, 19; Malachias, I, II.

[3] Pius XI, Encyclical, *"Divini Redemptoris"* (March 19, 1937)—*AAS*, XXIX, 82, 83. Translation from Koenig, *op. cit.*, n. 1228.

the sin of our first parents. For, as a matter of fact, these helps, whatever may be their nature, not only serve to advance civilization and culture; they also lead in an appropriate way to that thorough renewal of things which Christ the Saviour of men, contemplated and willed."[4]

ARTICLE II. THE CHURCH IS A JURIDICAL SOCIETY

There are many, especially among the Liberals, who admitting the legitimacy of the social form of the Church, nevertheless, deny her the right to exercise true jurisdiction over her members, for according to them the Church can merely persuade and exhort,[5] or, at the most, impose an obligation in *"foro conscientiae."* It is necessary, therefore, to study the constitution of the Church also from the juridical viewpoint; to establish first, that the Church is a juridical society; secondly, that the Church is juridically perfect.

The Church, according to the teaching of Christian philosophy, is a juridical society, because, besides having for its common purpose a good which is complete in its own sphere and all the necessary means to attain that end, she is invested by her Founder with the right to impose juridical obligations upon her members, who are strictly bound by justice to obey, and in case of negligence the Church is duly empowered to demand obedience through the action of the law, if necessary for the attainment of the common purpose pursued.[6]

The juridical perfection of the Church is by no means an arbitrary and liberal concession of nations, but is a fact that proceeds from the express and positive will of her Founder Who endowed his apostles and their successors with the supreme

---

[4] Leo XIII, Epistola, *"In Plurimis"* (May 5, 1888)—*ASS*, XX, 546.

[5] Pius VI, Const., *"Auctorem Fidei"*—Denzinger-Bannwart, n. 1507. The Church condemns as heretical the proposition which affirms: "abusum fore auctoritatis Ecclesiae, transferendo illam ultra limites doctrinae et morum, et eam extendendo ad res exteriores, et per vim exigendo id, quod pendet a persuasione et corde; multo minus ad eam pertinere, exigere per vim exteriorem subjectionem suis decretis. . . ."

[6] Pius IX, Encyclical, *"Quanta Cura"* (December 8, 1864)—Denzinger-Bannwart, n. 1697.

authority to govern the Church freely and independently of all earthly power. Amen I say to you, whatever you bind on earth shall be bound also in heaven. . . .[7]

To Peter, the supreme and visible head of the Church, Jesus said: "And I will give thee the keys of the kingdom of heaven; and whatever thou shalt bind on earth shall be bound in heaven, and whatever thou shalt loose on earth shall be loosed in heaven."[8] The word "key" both in its biblical and profane usage symbolizes supreme authority.[9] And the verbs "to bind and to loose" signify: the first, to declare authoritatively that a thing is obligatory; and, the second, to declare that a thing no longer enjoins moral obligation.[10]

Since Christ, however, built his Church not on Peter alone, but on all the apostles as a body, he, therefore, gave both to Peter and to the other apostles the supreme power to bind and to loose, i.e., legislative, judicial, and coercive powers; the laws made by the Church are not only binding in conscience, but, moreover, they can be enforced through compulsion and coercion, whenever the nature of the case requires it.

Another proof of the juridical constitution of the Church is clearly seen in the fact that the Church is necessary for salvation; outside the Church there is no salvation.[11] Unlike other societies which are freely established by men, the Church of Christ is a society whose membership is made obligatory by divine law, and, therefore, he who knowingly and voluntarily refrains from joining her is guilty of a grievous offense against the Saviour of mankind.[12] This conclusion is inescapable when one reads Christ's mandate: "Go into the whole world and preach the Gospel to every creature. He who believes and is

---

[7] St. Matth., XVIII, 18.

[8] St. Matth., XVI, 19-20.

[9] Zapalena, *De Ecclesia Christi, Pars Apologetica* (Romae: Apud Aedes Universitatis Gregorianae, 1940), p. 166.

[10] Zapalena, *op. cit.*, p. 168.

[11] Only those who are outside the Catholic Church through their own fault cannot expect salvation.

[12] Liberatore, M., *Le Droit Public de L'Eglise* (traduit de L'Italien par M. Aug. Onclair, Prêtre, Paris: Retaux-Bray, Libraire-Editeur, 1888), p. 17.

baptized shall be saved, but he who does not believe shall be condemned."[13] God had decreed that man should worship him and, thereby, attain his eternal happiness within the society established by himself. Hence, the Catholic Church is justly called the only saving church. To despise her is to despise Christ; to separate from her is to separate from Christ and to forfeit eternal salvation. This strict obligation which binds the faithful to attain their salvation, binds them in like manner to the membership of the only society founded by Christ as the necessary means to enter into the kingdom of heaven.[14]

It is clear, therefore, from the postive will of Christ and the very nature of the Church herself that the authority which she exercises is not limited merely to persuasion and exhortation, but also obliges both in the external and internal forum.

ARTICLE III. THE CHURCH IS A SOCIETY JURIDICALLY PERFECT

The Church, besides being a juridical society, is juridically perfect, i.e., she has for her purpose a good which is complete in its own sphere, all the necessary means, at least virtually if not actually, for achieving that end, and, finally, she is in her own order self-sufficient and independent. It is said that a society possesses virtually all that it needs for achieving its end, when it has the right to demand from other societies all the necessary means which actually it does not possess.

"In very truth Jesus Christ gave to his apostles unrestrained authority in regard to things sacred, together with the genuine and most true power of making laws, as also with the twofold right of judging, and of punishing, which flow from that power."[15]

In order to avoid any possible misunderstanding in this matter, it is wise to notice from the beginning that this power granted to the Church is only in the field of spiritual affairs, in all that pertains to the spiritual welfare of the souls, for in things merely temporal the Church has neither the desire nor the authority to

[13] St. Mark, XVI, 15-17.

[14] Cappello, *op. cit.*, p. 127.

[15] Leo XIII, Encyclical, "*Immortale Dei*" (November 1, 1885)—*ASS*, XVIII, 165. Translation from Wynne, *op. cit.*, p. 113.

interfere. "It is to the Church that God has assigned the charge of seeing to, and legislating for, all that concerns religion; of teaching all nations; of spreading the Christian faith as widely as possible; in short, of administering freely and without hindrance, in accordance with her own judgment, all matters that fall within its competence."[16]

There are several sacred texts in Holy Scripture which openly confirm the doctrine expounded above; that Christ gave his apostles full and independent power to make laws, to judge and to punish.

a) Legislative Power—This is the right to impose, in an obligatory form, that which is necessary for the attainment of the common purpose.[17] In other words, the legislative power makes laws which direct the common efforts of the members towards the common end. A law is "a rule prescribed by the sovereign of society to his subjects, either in order to lay an obligation upon them of doing or omitting certain things, under the commination of punishment; or to leave them at liberty to act or not in other things just as they think proper, and to secure to them, in this respect, the full enjoyment of their rights."[18]

This legislative power was conferred upon the apostles: "All power in heaven and on earth has been given to me. Go, therefore, and make disciples of all nations, baptizing them in the name of the Father . . . teaching them to observe all that I have commanded you; and behold, I am with you all days, even unto the consummation of the world."[19]

On another occasion he said: ". . . thou art Peter, and upon this rock I will build my Church, and the gates of hell shall not prevail against it. And I will give thee the keys of the kingdom of heaven: And whatever thou shalt bind on earth shall be bound in heaven, and whatever thou shalt loose on earth shall be also loosed in heaven."[20]

---

[16] Leo XIII, *ibid.*

[17] Cappello, *op. cit.*, n. 70. Tarquini, *Iuris Ecclesiastici Publici Institutiones* (4. ed., Romae: ex Typographia Polyglotta, 1875), n. 15.

[18] Burlamaqui, *The Principles of Natural and Political Law,* II, 65.

[19] St. Matth., XVIII, 18-20.

[20] St. Matth., XVI, 18-20.

It has been already stated that the word "key" symbolizes supreme authority, and the verb "to bind" the power to impose juridical obligations; however, both supreme authority symbolized by the word "key" and the right to exercise legislative power meant by the phrase "to bind" were expressly granted to Peter, the visible head of the Church. And to the apostles as a body, Jesus said: "Amen I say to you, whatever you shall bind on earth shall be bound also in heaven; and whatever you shall loose on earth shall be loosed also in heaven."[21] The same power that was given to Peter as Christ's vicar on earth is, hereby, given to all the apostles, to be exercised in harmony with his supreme authority.

If the Church were to be dependent upon the civil governments even in her legislation about spiritual matters, Jesus Christ should have addressed these words to the civil rulers and not to the apostles who are the constituted rulers of the Church.

The endowment of the Church with legislative power is manifested in her actual use of it. I) The acts of the apostles: As the apostles are the authentic interpreters not merely of the divine revelation itself, but also of the main sources thereof, their teaching and practices in this matter constitute, thereby, a forceful, nay, an evident proof of the existence of this legislative power in the Church of God. As a matter of fact, the apostles passed laws not only when assembled in council, but as individuals as well. In Jerusalem they decreed disciplinary laws in these words: "For the Holy Spirit, and we have decided to lay no further burden upon you, but this indispensable one, that you abstain from things sacrificed to idols and from blood and from what is strangled . . .; keep yourselves from these things. . . ."[22] These prohibitions were necessarily enforced in those days, because of the scandal that would otherwise be given to the Jews newly converted to Christianity. For, according to the Mosaic law it was a sin not to abstain from these things.

St. Paul acting alone legislated several ecclesiastical enactments, v.g., about matrimony. "For to the rest I say, not the

---

[21] St. Matth., XVIII, 18.
[22] Acts, XV, 28, 29.

Lord: If any brother has an unbelieving wife and she consents to live with him, let him not put her away. And if any woman has an unbelieving husband, and he consents to live with her, let her not put away her husband. For the unbelieving husband is sanctified by the believing wife, and the unbelieving wife is sanctified by the believing husband. But if the unbeliever departs, let him depart. For a brother or sister is not under bondage in such cases, but God called us to peace."[23] II) The present code of canon law is an evident proof of this legislative power of the Church. The code of canon law prescribes the following: 1) "The Catholic Church possesses, by divine institution, the power of jurisdiction or government. This power is twofold: that of the external forum, and that of the internal forum, or forum of conscience. . . ."[24]

2) "As the successor to the primacy of St. Peter, the Roman Pontiff has not only the primacy of honor, but also supreme and full power of jurisdiction over the universal Church, in matters of faith and morals as well as in those pertaining to the discipline and government of the Church throughout the whole world."

3) "This power is episcopal, or ordinary and immediate, and extends over each and every church, and over each and every pastor as well as over the faithful, and is independent of all human authority."[25]

4) "The bishop has the right and the duty to govern the diocese both in spiritual and temporal affairs, and to this end he possesses legislative, judicial, and coercive power which must be exercised according to the precepts of the Sacred Canons. The laws of the bishop begin to bind immediately when promulgated, unless he provides otherwise in the same laws."[26]

b) Judicial Power—This is the right to declare authentically the true sense of the law, and to judge whether the actions of the members are, or are not in conformity with the law.[27] The

---

[23] I Corinthians, VII, 12, 15.

[24] Canon 196. Translation from Woywod, *op. cit.*, I, n. 149.

[25] Canon 218, § 1; § 2. Translation from Woywod, *op. cit.*, I, n. 171.

[26] Canon 335. Translation from Woywod, *op. cit.*, I, n. 246.

[27] Tarquini, *op. cit.*, n. 20.

judicial power naturally flows from the right to enact laws. If the Church can make laws, she must also and necessarily have the right to declare the definite sense of her laws; otherwise, the numberless doubts, which would easily arise about the authentic sense of the laws due to the diversity of viewpoints of the members, would certainly render the laws entirely useless. "Lex dubia non obligat."

That the Church has this power is clearly seen in the Holy Scripture. "But if thy brother sin against thee, go and show him his fault, between thee and him alone. If he listen to thee, thou hast won thy brother. But if he do not listen to thee, take with thee one or two more so that on the word of two or three witnesses every word may be confirmed. And if he refuse to hear them, appeal to the Church, but if he refuse to hear even the Church, let him be to thee as the heathen and the publican."[28]

And St. Paul makes use of his judicial power: "I indeed, absent in body, but present in spirit, have already, as though present, passed judgment in the name of the Lord Jesus on the one who has so acted—you and my spirit gathered together with the power of our Lord Jesus—to deliver such a one over to Satan for the destruction of the flesh, that his spirit may be saved in the day of our Lord Jesus Christ."[29] The code of canon law thus ordains:

1) "The Church has the inherent and exclusive right to judge: I) cases which relate to spiritual matters, or to temporal matters annexed to spiritual; II) violations of ecclesiastical laws, and all other actions in which sin is implicated, in so far as the decision on the guilt and the infliction of ecclesiastical penalties are concerned; III) all civil and criminal cases of persons who enjoy the privilege of the ecclesiastical forum, as defined by canons 120, 614, and 680.

2) "In those cases in which the civil courts have concurrent jurisdiction with the ecclesiastical courts—the so-called cases of the mixed forum—prevention holds good, that is, whichever court

[28] St. Matth., XVIII, 15, 18.

[29] I Corinthians, V, 3-5.

first accepts the complaint or prosecutes the offender, has the right to judge the case."[30]

3) In regard to marriage: "Matrimonial cases between baptized persons belong by proper and exclusive right to the ecclesiastical judge."[31]

4) "Cases concerning the mere civil consequences of marriage belong exclusively to the civil court, if they are brought to court as principal actions (cfr. canon 1016); but, if they are incidental or accessory to a case on the validity or licitness of marriage, the ecclesiastical judge is competent to try and decide these cases."[32]

The Church, therefore, by the express will of her Founder possesses judicial power; this fact is evidenced by the acts of the apostles and the continual teaching and legislation of the Church herself.

c) Coercive Power—This is the right to demand obedience through compulsion, and to inflict punishment upon disobedience to the laws.[33]

That the Church holds and exercises this power clearly appears in the Gospels, and in the present legislation of the Church. The Gospels: "And if he refuse to hear them, appeal to the Church, but if he refuse to hear even the Church, let him to be to thee as the heathen and the publican."[34] Therefore, according to this passage of Holy Scripture, an erring brother, if he persists in his sinful conduct, notwithstanding the repeated admonition of the ecclesiastical authorities, can be compelled by the Church to due emendation, to the extent of imposing on him the punishment of excommunication.

The present legislation of the Church: "The Church has the innate and proper right, independent of all human authority, to punish her guilty subjects with both spiritual and temporal penalties."[35] This power is natural to her constitution, i.e., given

---

[30] Canon 1553, § 1. Translation from Woywod, *op. cit.*, II, n. 1547.

[31] Canon 1960. Translation from Woywod, *op. cit.*, II, n. 1866.

[32] Canon 1961. Translation from Woywod, *op. cit.*, II, n. 1867.

[33] Tarquini, *op. cit.*, n. 21. Cappello, *op. cit.*, n. 77.

[34] St. Matth., XVIII, 17, 18. The heathen and the publican were for the Jews the excommunicated.

[35] Canon 2214, § 1. Translation from Woywod, *op. cit.*, II, n. 2050.

by her Founder; proper, not delegated by somebody; and independent, not subject to any civil authority.[36]

ARTICLE IV. THE CHURCH AS A SOCIETY IS A LEGAL PERSON

It is to the Church that our Lord committed the perpetuation of his mission on earth. "In this which he founded and in the very founding of that Church, what did Christ have in mind as his aim? This, precisely, was his desire—to transmit to it that very mission and that same mandate which he had received from his father, that it might be continued forever. That was what he decided should be done. That was what he actually did."[37]

Because of this mission to secure for its members, besides their personal sanctification, a good which is common to all and is perpetual, the Church as society was made *"subiectum sui iuris,"* i.e., it was endowed with the right to "possess in itself and by itself, through the will and loving kindness of its Founder, all needful provisions for its maintenance and action."[38]

With these words the Pope declares that the inviolability of the Church in her rights to existence and action is a divine—positive act of liberality on the part of her Founder. The code of canon law clearly states that the Catholic Church and the Holy See are by divine institution legal persons.[39] The Church is, therefore, a moral or legal person; person, in analogy to the natural person; and moral, to differentiate her from the physical one, for the Church is the moral union of the faithful. Like a natural person the Church is inviolable in her rights. There are many canons in the code which safeguard her rights, freedom of action and independence as a legal person, as a perfect society.[40]

The Church like the State exists *"sui iuris"* independently of all other societies, and freely exercises her rights as a natural person

---

[36] Vermeersch-Creusen, *op. cit.*, III, n. 400.

[37] Leo XIII, Encyclical, *"Satis Cognitum"* (June 29, 1896)—*ASS*, XXVIII, 712.

[38] Leo XIII, Encyclical, *"Immortale Dei"* (November 1, 1885)—*ASS*, XVIII, 165. Translation from Wynne, *op. cit.*, p. 112.

[39] Canon 100, § 1.

[40] Canons 1495; 1499; 1518; 1556; 1557; 2214; 1352; 1384.

does. "The Church, therefore, possesses the right to exist and to protect herself by institutions and laws in accordance with her nature. And since she not only is a perfect society in herself, but superior to every other society of human growth, she resolutely refuses, prompted alike by right and duty, to link herself to any mere party and to subject herself to the fleeting exigencies of politics."[41]

---

[41] Leo XIII, Encyclical, *"Immortale Dei"* (November 1, 1885)—*ASS*, XVIII, 387. Translation from Wynne, *op. cit.*, p. 196.

CHAPTER VII

Ecclesiastical Authority

ARTICLE I. NOTION OF ECCLESIASTICAL AUTHORITY

> Over this mighty multitude God has himself set rulers with power to govern; and he has willed that one should be the head of all, and the chief and unerring teacher of truth. . . .[1]

The Church under her divine constitution exercises a twofold authority over her members; the authority of ordination, and the authority of jurisdiction.[2] The present consideration is strictly limited to the power of jurisdiction which the Roman Pontiff, as supreme Pastor of the universal Church, exercises directly and immediately over all the faithful. "Jurisdiction, in general, is the power of ruling the subjects, for the purpose of achieving the aim of a perfect society.[3] This is the power which the ruler of every perfect society has in ruling the subjects, exercising thereby, fully and independently, the threefold function of supreme authority, legislative, judicial and coercive.

Ecclesiastical jurisdiction, therefore, "is the power which the Church has by divine institution to rule those who are baptized for the purpose of achieving the supernatural end."[4]

ARTICLE II. NATURE OF ECCLESIASTICAL AUTHORITY

The Church being, by divine institution, a society juridically perfect has, like the State, a ruling authority. The ruling power

---

[1] Leo XIII, Encyclical, *"Immortale Dei"* (November 1, 1885)—*ASS,* XVIII, 164, 165. Translation from Wynne, *op. cit.*, p. 112.

[2] Canons 196; 210; 948.

[3] Coronata, *Institutiones Iuris Canonici* (5 vols., Vols. I, II, 2. ed., 1939; Vols., III, IV, V, 1933-1936, Taurini: Marietti), I, 275.

[4] Vermeersch-Creusen, *Epitome Iuris Canonici,* I, n. 312. Translation by the writer.

in the Church, unlike that in the State, is supernatural and spiritual. The reasons for these qualifications in the authority of the Church are: a) she has for her immediate author God himself. "Peace be with you," Christ said to his apostles. "As the Father has sent me, I also send you."[5] She derives her origin directly and immediately from God as her immediate source, while the civil power, though it comes also from God, derives its origin from God only by way of nature.[6]

b) the objects upon which the authority of the Church is exercised are spiritual and supernatural. The Church has been commissioned, as a matter of fact, to administer the sacraments and to govern the faithful in matters of faith and morals. She is concerned with temporal things only in as much as these are annexed to spiritual things, or are necessary for the attainment of her end which is purely spiritual, and supernatural.[7]

c) finally, the authority of the Church is spiritual and supernatural, because of the purpose for which she was instituted. The apostles and their successors were sent forth into the world to teach, to baptize, and to govern those who believe, that they may be sanctified, and thereby attain their eternal happiness.

For the very reasons given above, the ecclesiastical authority is nobler than that of the State. "And just as the end at which the Church aims is by far the noblest of ends, so is its authority the most exalted of all authority, nor can it be looked as inferior to the civil power, or in any manner dependent upon it."[8]

ARTICLE III. FORM OF GOVERNMENT IN THE CHURCH

Not only does the right to govern in the Church have its origin from God, who directly and immediately has given the supreme

[5] St. John, XX, 21.

[6] Bossuet, *Controverse, Œuvres Complètes, Defensio Declarationis Cleri Gallicani*, XXXIX, XL, 268, says: "Quaeres quid iam intersit sacerdotalem et civilem potestatem, si utraque est a Deo? Multum per omnem modum . . . quia sacerdotalis potestas in lege et in Evangelio a Deo ipso praesente . . . civile autem imperium, quamquam suo modo a Deo vel inditum vel institutum sit, haud pari praesentiae divinae Maiestatis. . . ."

[7] Ottaviani, *op. cit.*, I, 211.

[8] Leo XIII, Encyclical, *"Immortale Dei"* (November 1, 1885)—*ASS*, XVIII, 165. Translation from Wynne, *op. cit.*, pp. 112, 113.

authority to Peter, the visible head of the Church, but also the form of government therein, unlike that in the State, has been expressly determined by God himself, and, therefore, it is completely independent of the choice of man.[9]

Peter and his successors hold and exercise the supreme authority over all the faithful.[10] This supreme authority is, therefore, exercised by one person, the Roman Pontiff, who presides over the whole Church; makes laws, and judges all without any exception, while no person can judge him.[11] This form of government is undoubtedly an absolute Monarchy, although it is marked by something of aristocracy and democracy: of aristocracy, not because the supreme authority in the Church is divided among many, but because, by divine institution, the Pope together with the bishops rules the Church with parallel power; the bishops, subordinate to the Roman Pontiff in their respective dioceses; of democracy, inasmuch as the highest dignitary in the Church can be chosen from the people.[12]

SUMMARY

The redeemer of the human race in order to perpetuate his mission on earth has established the Church, a society in which it is divinely ordained that man should be a member. Man has a divinely-imposed obligation to pursue his perfection both in body and in soul. The first would be his temporal prosperity, attainable in the civil society, and the latter, his eternal happiness,

[9] St. Matth., XVI, 18, 19; St. John, XXI, 16, 18.

[10] Conc. Vat. (sess. iv, c. I, de Ecclesia Christi, cf. Denzinger-Bannwart, nn. 1823, 1824) says: "Si quis dixerit igitur, beatum Petrum apostolum non esse a Christo Domino constitutum omnium apostolorum principem et totius Ecclesiae militantis invisibile caput, vel eumdem honoris tantum, non autem verae propriaeque iurisdictionis primatum ab eodem Domino Nostro Jesu Christo directe et immediate accepisse, a. sit."

"Si quis dixerit non esse ex ipsius Christi institutione seu iure divino, ut beatus Petrus in primatu super universam ecclesiam, habeat perpetuos successores, a. sit."

[11] Canon 1556: "Prima Sedes a nemine judicatur."

[12] Cappello, *Summa Iuris Ecclesiastici Publici*, p. 499 (footnote).

attainable in the Church. For this reason the Church, like the State, was endowed by her Founder with all the necessary means to attain her purpose. For an effective co-ordination of all the efforts of the members towards the common good a ruling power, perfect and supreme, was given to her. The Church by reason of her members, means, purpose, and authority, is a visible, public, necessary and perfect society. What has the State in regard to its perfection as a society which is not found in the Church?

CHAPTER VIII

The Juridical Relations Between the State and the Church

ARTICLE I. FIRST PRINCIPLE

The preceding chapters dealt with the social and juridical nature of the only two perfect societies on earth. The intention of the present chapter is to present the principles which must govern the relations between the Church and the State. It is not difficult to determine, in the light of Christian philosophy, the fundamental norms upon which to base the juridical relations between these two institutions, to which the general welfare of man has been entrusted. "The Almighty, therefore, has given the charge of the human race to two powers, the ecclesiastical and the civil, one being set over divine, the other over human things."[1]

God has made man a social being, composed of body and soul. It is divinely ordained that he should live in society in order to attain the purpose for which he was created. For this reason the all-wise Creator created two societies, corresponding to man's nature, one spiritual, the Church, and the other temporal, the State, of which man is a member. Each of these two societies has its own proper structure, duties, rights and power.[2]

And as the institution of the Church and the State, together with their respective duties, rights and power, does not rest with the will of man, likewise the principles regulating the relations which must exist between them are set independently of

---

[1] Leo XIII, Encyclical, *"Immortale Dei"* (November 1, 1885)—*ASS*, XVIII, 166. Translation from Wynne, *op. cit.*, p. 114.

[2] Nicolaus I (*in epistola 86 ad Michaelem Imperatorem*): "ultra sibi nec Imperator iura Pontificatus arripuit, nec Pontifex nomen Imperatorum usurpavit, quoniam Christus Jesus sic actibus propriis et dignitatibus distinctis officia potestatis utriusque discrevit." Cf. Denzinger-Bannwart, n. 333.

the choice of man. "But inasmuch as each of these two powers has authority over the same subjects . . . therefore God, who foresees all things, and who is the author of these two powers, has marked out the course of each in the right correlation to the other. There must, accordingly, exist, between these two powers, a certain connection, which may be compared to the union of the soul and body in man."[3]

Catholic authors have always compared to the union of the soul and the body in man the harmony that must exist in the relations between the Church and a Catholic State. A Catholic state is that whose population is morally Catholic.[4] It is not necessary that the whole legislation of the nation should be at the same time based upon Catholic principles.[5] Whenever harmonious relations exist between these two societies things have prospered, and "were this not so, deplorable contentions and conflicts would often arise, and not unfrequently men, like travelers at the meeting of two roads, would hesitate in anxiety and doubt, not knowing what course to follow. Two powers would be commanding contrary things, and it would be dereliction of duty to disobey either of the two."[6] The Catholic doctrine in this matter can be enunciated in the following principles:

> Whatever, therefore, in things human is of a sacred character, whatever belongs either for its own nature or by reason of the end to which it is referred, to the salvation of souls, or to the worship of God, is subject to the power and judgment of the Church.[7]

In the spiritual order the Church is exclusively and independently competent. This means by implication that the ecclesiastical authority is strictly limited to the spiritual sphere, and,

---

[3] Leo XIII, *ibid.*

[4] Cappello, *op. cit.*, n. 324.

[5] Cavagnis (*Institutiones Iuris Publici Ecclesiastici*, p. 247) asserts: "Civilis societas catholica est quae constat membris catholicis, et principia catholica agnoscit ut normam legislationis."

[6] Leo XIII, Encyclical, "*Immortale Dei*" (November 1, 1885)—*ASS*, XVIII, 166. Translation from Wynne, *op. cit.*, p. 114.

[7] Leo XIII, *ibid.*, pp. 166, 167. Translation from Wynne, *op. cit.*, p. 115.

therefore, has no power over merely temporal things. A thing is merely temporal, if it is directly and immediately intended to attain temporal well-being.[8]

That the Church was not given power over merely temporal things appears evident. Christ, interrogated by Pilate about his kingdom, said: "My Kingdom is not of this world. If my Kingdom were of this world, my followers would have fought that I might not be delivered to the Jews. But, as it is, my Kingdom is not from here."[9] The kingdom of Christ on earth is undoubtedly the Church which is, therefore, according to the positive statement of our Lord, not a temporal, but a spiritual society.

The restricted sphere of the Church's jurisdiction also appears evident from the command of Christ to Peter: "And I say to thee, thou art Peter, and upon this rock I will build my church. . . . And I will give thee the keys of the kingdom of heaven; and whatever thou shalt bind on earth shall be bound in heaven, whatever thou shalt loose on earth shall be loosed in heaven."[10] For Christ did not promise in granting this commission the keys of a temporal kingdom, but those of the spiritual one, and, thus manifested that he was conferring not a temporal power, but a spiritual one.

On the other hand, Leo XIII says: "No one can, however, without risk to faith, foster any doubt as to the Church alone having been invested with such power of governing souls as to exclude altogether the civil authority. In truth it was not to Caesar, but to Peter that Jesus Christ entrusted the keys of the kingdom of heaven."[11]

"Hence it is the Church, and not the State, that is to be man's guide to heaven. It is to the Church that God has assigned the charge of seeing to, and legislating for, all that concerns religion; of teaching all nations; of spreading the Christian faith as widely as possible; in short, of administering freely and

---

[8] Cappello, *op. cit.*, n. 273.

[9] St. John, XVIII, 36, 37.

[10] St. Matth., XVI, 18-19.

[11] Leo XIII, Encyclical, *Sapientiae Christianae* (1890)—*ASS*, XXII, 396. Translation from Wynne, *The Great Encyclical Letters of Leo XIII*, p. 196.

without hindrance, in accordance with her own judgment, all matters that fall within its competence."[12]

To confirm this, the code of canon law states in numerous canons the exclusive right of the Church in spiritual things. For example, in regard to the sacrament of matrimony it says: "The marriage of the baptized persons is governed not only by the divine, but also by canon law. The civil power is competent only to legislate concerning merely civil effects of such marriages."[13]

Merely temporal power, or civil authority, in the Church would prove pernicious rather than useful to the attainment of her objective. It is not necessary, because the Church, in virtue of her spiritual power, can dispose of all things even temporal, if these by reason of the end to which they are referred, are related to the salvation of the souls.

It would prove pernicious, because the possession of merely temporal things easily diverts the attention of men from the spiritual ones, and, thereby, hinders the attainment of the purpose of the Church. Jesus Christ came into this world to teach men to despise worldly things.

There have been in the Church, especially in the medieval age, some learned authors who advocated the possession by the Church of direct power over the State, that is, over temporal things considered as such.[14] This doctrine asserted that the Roman Pontiff is the centre of all authority on earth, that in him all power has been deposited, and that therefore, the civil rulers of nations are but the vicars of the Pope. To the Pope is attributed the exclusive privilege to judge the civil rulers, and to deprive them of their power even for merely temporal and material reasons. They tried to prove this by some passages of Holy Scripture. In our day, no author in the Catholic Church

---

[12] Leo XIII, Encyclical, *Immortale Dei* (1885)—*ASS,* XVIII, 165. Translation from Wynne, *op. cit.,* p. 113.

[13] Canon 1016. Translation from Woywod, *op. cit.,* I, n. 980.

[14] Aegidius Romanus (1244-1316), *De Potestate Ecclesiastica* (edited by Richard S. Weimar, Herman Boehlaus, 1929), cc. V-X; Alvarus Pelagius (1350) *De Planctu Ecclesiae* (Venetiis, F. Sansovini et Sociorum, 1560), lib., I, cc. 13, 41, 44, 46, 57 and 68.

maintains this idea, for according to the principle just enunciated the State is independent and supreme in the temporal order.

ARTICLE II. SECOND PRINCIPLE

> Whatever is to be ranged under the civil and political order is rightly subject to the civil authority. Jesus Christ himself has given command "that what is Caesar's is to be rendered to Caesar, and that what belongs to God is to be rendered to God."[15]

It has been repeatedly stated in the foregoing pages that the Almighty has entrusted the general welfare of mankind to two perfect societies, the Church and the State, the former being set over divine and the latter, over human things. It is the will of the Creator that each of these two societies be supreme in its own province. The civil power is directly intended to attain temporal prosperity; for this reason it is exclusively competent in the temporal order, i.e., it is not subject to any other authority of its own kind. The Church has no power, direct or indirect, over the affairs of the State, so long as these are not pernicious to religion and morality. For if the Church could duly interfere in merely civil affairs, then the State would not be a supreme and independent society. It is, therefore, within the competence of the State to employ all temporal means necessary to attain its aim. It is to be emphasized, however, that this supremacy of the State is exclusively in the merely temporal order; it is, by no means, in every respect unlimited. There are cases in which civil rulers may be directed, assisted and even corrected by the Church for the sake of a higher and eternal purpose.[16]

"It is true that the actions of the State, whether in the field of legislation of administration, have moral aspects, inasmuch as they are human actions; therefore, they are in some manner subject to the Church as the interpreter of the moral law."[17]

---

[15] Leo XIII, Encyclical, *"Immortale Dei"* (November 1, 1885)—*ASS*, XVIII, 167. Translation from Wynne, *op. cit.*, p. 115.

[16] Suarez, *op. cit.*, XXIV, 224, 225.

[17] Ryan and Boland, *Catholic Principles of Politics* (Revised Edition of *The State and the Church*, New York: The Macmillan Company, 1941), p. 324.

This subjection of the State to the Church is indirect, inasmuch as the Church interferes in temporal affairs not *"per se"* and *"propter se,"* but for the sake of another higher purpose.

Many authors in political science advocate that the State is omnipotent, that it is the only supreme society on earth. According to this theory, the Church is merely one of the many private societies existing within and subordinate to the State; it is not independent, nor has it any province that is exclusively its own. This theory, as it is thus stated, has been condemned by the Church.[18]

ARTICLE III. THIRD PRINCIPLE

> The Church exercises indirect power over temporal things. . . .[19]

This proposition is implicitly meant in the following statement of Leo XIII: "Whatever, therefore, in things human is of a sacred character, whatever belongs either of its own nature or by reason of the end to which it is referred, to the salvation of souls, or to the worship of God, is subject to the power and judgment of the Church."[20]

This power of the Church, although indirectly exercised over temporal things, is true jurisdiction with the threefold function of supreme authority, legislative, judicial and coercive. It is called indirect, because it affects temporal things only when and so far as they have some relation to faith and morals, and thus to the salvation of the souls.[21] It is really a spiritual power though it affects the temporal order, and this for three reasons: a) it is for the spiritual mission of the Church; b) it is for the

[18] Pius IX, *Syllabus,* n. 39. Cf. Denzinger-Bannwart, n. 1739.

[19] Cappello, *Summa Iuris Publici Ecclesiastici,* p. 299. "Ecclesiae competit potestas indirecta in res temporales. . . ."

[20] Leo XIII, Encyclical, *"Immortale Dei"* (November 1, 1885)—*ASS,* 166, 167. Translation from Wynne, *op. cit.,* p. 115.

[21] Suarez, *op. cit.,* XXIV, lib. III, 244, 245. "Indirecta quae solum nascitur ex directione ad finem altiorem et ad superiorem ac excellentiorem potestatem pertinentem."

spiritual guidance of men; c) it is intended solely for the spiritual welfare of mankind.[22]

To have a clear understanding of this indirect power of the Church Monsignor Ryan gives us this supposition: "Suppose that the people of Russia were suddenly converted to the faith of the Roman Catholic Church, and that they appealed to the Pope for an authoritative judgment as to whether they were to support the government of Lenin and Trotzky. Obviously this is a moral, not a legal question. We will suppose that the Russians place more confidence in the authoritative judgment of the Catholic Church. . . . After due consideration of all the facts the Pope decides that the people of Russia are under no moral obligation to continue their support of the Communistic Regime. In consequence of the acceptance of this decision by the Russian people, the government is unable to continue. In effect the Pope has deposed Lenin and Trotzky."[23]

In this case the Church, as the guardian and interpreter of the moral law, has the right to interfere in civil affairs, because they involve at times an intimate relation to religion and morality.

The possession by the Church of indirect power over the State is a common doctrine of the Fathers, Doctors, Theologians and Canonists of the Catholic Church. St. Bellarmine and Suarez, however, are the outstanding doctors who have explained and defended this doctrine systematically.[24]

At first sight, the indirect subordination of the State to the Church seems contrary to the principle already established that God, for the orderly government of mankind, has delegated his authority to two perfect societies, each independently and exclusively competent to regulate the affairs of its subjects within its own province. But considering attentively the purpose for

---

[22] Ottaviani, *Institutiones Iuris Publici Ecclesiastici,* n. 305.

[23] Ryan and Boland, *op. cit.,* p. 327.

[24] St. Bellarmine, *De Controversis: De Potestate Temporali Pontificis,* t. I, lib. V; *De Translatione Imperii Romani de Graccis ad Francos,* t. I, lib. I-III; *De Potestate Romani Pontificis contra Barclaium,* t. V, c. I-XLII. Suarez, *De Legibus,* lib. IV, c. 9. Cf. St. Bellarmine, *Opera Omnia* (ed. nova juxta Venetam, 8 vols., Napoli: C. Pedone Lauriel Editor, 1721), I, V.

which God has established these two institutions and for which he has given to each his authority, it appears reasonable that the society whose objective and power are in the lower category in dignity and importance should be subordinated, at least indirectly, to that which is superior in the dignity of its nature and end. The State was established as supreme authority for the temporal welfare of man in this world, while the Church was founded by our Lord for the spiritual welfare of man also in this world, but especially to lead him to his eternal happiness. The spiritual and eternal interest of man is, however, more important than his temporal and material happiness; it follows naturally from this consideration that the Church to which the spiritual welfare of man is entrusted, is nobler in dignity and importance than the State which promotes the merely temporal well-being.[25]

Besides, the Church is a perfect society, and as such it must have all the means necessary to attain its end. But to attain its purpose the right to dispose of temporal things is necessary because, otherwise, as St. Bellarmine remarks, Princes unfavorable towards the Church could freely foster heresy and menace the very foundation of religion in a State.[26] Therefore, the Church must have and in reality has this power over the State.

The theory of directive power limited the power of the Church over the State to mere guidance and direction. The Church has the right to declare that a law is morally binding or not, to teach the civil rulers their obligations, to exhort them to a diligent fulfillment thereof, and in case of negligence to reprimand them. Civil rulers are by divine institution not subject to any ecclesiastical authority in the temporal order.[27]

Those who maintained this theory assert that: a) they do not see the reason why the Church should have indirect power over

---

[25] Billot, *Tractatus de Ecclesia Christi*, II, pp. 76-78.

[26] St. Bellarmine, *De Romano Pontifice*, t. I, lib. V, c. VII, p. 532.

[27] Bossuet (*Defensio Declarationis Cleri Gallicani*, lib. II, c. V) says: "Reges et Principes in temporalibus nulli ecclesiasticae potestati Dei ordinatione subiici, neque auctoritate clavium Ecclesiae directe vel indirecte deponi, aut illorum subditos eximi a fide atque obedientia, ac praestito iuramento fidelitatis sacramento solvi posse."

the State; b) indirect power is in reality the same as direct power; c) the merely directive power is enough for the Church to attain its purpose.[28]

This theory is not only opposed to the common teaching of the Catholic church, but is expressly included in the *"Syllabus,"* or the collection of modern errors condemned by Pius IX.[29]

ARTICLE IV. FOURTH PRINCIPLE

> In matters, however, of mixed jurisdiction, it is in the highest degree consonant to nature, as also to the designs of God, that so far from one of the powers separating itself from the other, or still less coming into conflict with it, complete harmony, such as is suitable to the end for which each power exists, should be preserved between them.[30]

A matter of mixed jurisdiction is that thing which, remaining one and the same, although possessing different relations, pertains directly and at the same time to both spiritual and temporal welfare, and, thereby, belongs to the jurisdiction of both the Church and the State.[31]

Matters of joint jurisdiction may be divided into two groups: 1) a thing may be of mixed jurisdiction *"per se"* or *"per accidens."* It is such "per se" when, by its own nature, it pertains to the objective of both societies; *"per accidens"* when it tends to the benefit of both societies, not by its own nature, but by some circumstances usually imposed by the will of man, v.g., the violation of a contract. In the latter case, this matter falls under the jurisdiction of the Church, not by its own nature, but because sin is implicated. It is a mixed affair *"per accidens"* in regard to the Church.[32] 2) matters of joint jurisdiction may be natural

[28] Ottaviani, *op. cit.,* II, 148.

[29] Pius IX, *Syllabus,* prop. n. 29, "Ecclesia vis inferendae potestatem non habet neque potestatem ullam temporalem directam vel indirectam." Cf. Denzinger-Bannwart, n. 1724.

[30] Leo XIII, Encyclical, *"Immortale Dei"* (November 1, 1885)—*ASS,* XVIII, 174. Translation from Wynne, *op. cit.,* p. 126.

[31] Leo XIII, *loc. cit.*

[32] Cappello, *op. cit.,* n. 342.

or supernatural according as their nature is within or beyond the natural sphere. Some matters, although by nature within the natural order, are, however, made supernatural by the will of God, v.g., matrimony which previously was only the natural union of one man and one woman, was raised by our Lord to the dignity of a sacrament, a supernatural matter.[33]

The effects deriving from the supernatural matters of mixed jurisdiction are in turn divisible into two groups: 1) separable or inseparable according as they derive naturally and necessarily therefrom or not. 2) spiritual or temporal. Temporal effects, if inseparable, are denominated civil effects, and if they are separable, merely civil.[34] For example, in matrimony, sanctifying grace and the right to graces necessary for conjugal life are the spiritual and supernatural effects; mutual rights and duties, and the legitimacy of the children are the inseparable effects of matrimony, while the dowry, the right of succession as to inheritance and to other civil privileges of the parties are the separable, or merely civil effects.

It is to be noticed that supernatural things are classified as of mixed jurisdiction only in regard to their effects; in themselves they are exclusively within the competence of the Church.

In the light of the principle of joint jurisdiction, the following conclusions can be stated: 1) the Church and the State must not make laws in these matters without mutual understanding. Since the two powers legislate upon the same things and for the same subjects, easily contradictory laws would result from one-sided legislation, enacted without mutual consultation.

"But when anything has to be settled which for different reasons and in a different way concerns both powers, necessity and public utility demand that an agreement shall be effected between them, without which an uncertain and unstable condition of things will be the result, totally inconsistent with the peace either of Church or State."[35] 2) the State has no right at all to make

[33] Ottaviani, *op. cit.,* II, n. 327.

[34] Cappello, *op. cit.,* n. 343.

[35] Leo XIII, Encyclical, *"Nobilissima Gallorum Gens"* (February 8, 1884) —*ASS,* XVI, 244, 245. Translation from Koenig, *op. cit.,* n. 45.

laws about supernatural mixed matters, together with their inseparable effects; it is, however, free to legislate about their separable effects, that is, about the merely civil ones.[36]

ARTICLE V. FIFTH PRINCIPLE

> All who rule, therefore, should hold in honor the Holy Name of God, and one of their chief duties must be to favor religion, to protect it, to shield it under the credit and sanction of the laws, and neither to organize nor enact any measure that may compromise its safety.[37]

The State is synonymous with those who represent the civil society, those who hold and exercise the supreme authority in a nation.[38] Two obligations, one positive and the other negative, on the part of the civil society, are clearly enunciated in the fifth principle.

The positive obligation of the State: The Christian State is bound to make public profession of religion. The reason is that the civil society is as dependent upon God as any individual man. "Nature and reason, which command every individual devoutly to worship God in holiness, because we belong to him and must return to him since from him we came, bind also the civil community by a like law. For men living together in society are under the power of God no less than individuals are, and society, not less than individuals, owes gratitude to God, who gave it being and maintains it, and whose ever-bounteous goodness enriches it with countless blessings."[39]

"As we are each of us admonished by the very voice of nature to worship God in piety and holiness, as the Giver unto us of life and of all that is good therein, so also and for the same reason, nations and States are bound to worship him; and therefore it

---

[36] Ottaviani, *op. cit.*, II, n. 330.

[37] Leo XIII, Encyclical, *"Immortale Dei"* (November 1, 1885)—*ASS*, XVIII, 164. Translation from Wynne, *op. cit.*, p. 111.

[38] Billot, *op. cit.*, II, 91, 92.

[39] Leo XIII, Encyclical, *"Immortale Dei"* (November 1, 1885)—*ASS*, XVIII, 163. Translation from Wynne, *op. cit.*, p. 110.

is clear that those who would absolve society from all religious duty act not only unjustly but also with ignorance and folly."[40]

Therefore, the State, no less than individuals, is bound to make public profession of religion. It, however, really and publicly professes religion when its laws and other institutions are imbued with religious principles.[41] Although the civil society is morally compelled to profess religion, it is by no means free to choose any kind of worship. "Since, then, no one is allowed to be remiss in the service due to God, and since the chief duty of all man is to cling to religion in both its teaching and practice—not such religion as they may have a preference for, but the religion which God enjoins, and which certain and most clear marks show to be the only one true religion [is to be professed]. . . ."[42]

This same obligation which binds individuals to worship God in that way which he has revealed to be his will binds in like manner the State which in the terms of Billot is just an amplification of the individual man.[43]

Hence, "it is a public crime to act as though there were no God. So, too, is it a sin in the State not to have care for religion, as a something beyond its scope, or as of no practical benefit; or out of many forms of religion to adopt that one which chimes in with the fancy; for we are bound absolutely to worship God in that way which he has shown to be his will."[44]

It is not within the intention of this dissertation to prove which is the true religion, since it is taken for granted that in a Catholic State both the rulers and the citizens, at least the majority if not all, are fully convinced that the Catholic religion is the true one. To this kind of State Leo XIII refers when he firmly states that the principle known as the union of Church and State should be the basis of the relations between them.

---

[40] Leo XIII, Encyclical, "*Humanum Genus*" (April 20, 1884)—*ASS*, XVI, 429. Translation from Wynne, *op. cit.*, p. 98.

[41] Billot, *op. cit.*, II, 92.

[42] Leo XIII, Encyclical, "*Immortale Dei*" (November 1, 1885)—*ASS*, XVIII, 163. Translation from Wynne, *op. cit.*, p. 110.

[43] Billot (*op. cit.*, II, 93) says: "Status nihil aliud est quam homo associatione amplificatus, in aciem communitatis instructus. . . ."

[44] Leo XIII, Encyclical, "*Immortale Dei*" (November 1, 1885)—*ASS*, XVIII, 163, 164. Translation from Wynne, *op. cit.*, p. 111.

In virtue of this principle the civil society is bound not only to recognize the Catholic religion as the State-religion and to protect it, but also and above all, to provide her in the temporal order with all the material means necessary to carry on her mission to its perfection. The Catholic Church is not an entirely spiritual and divine society; it is at the same time a human community. Thus, Pius XI, speaking of the imminent threat of communism to the Church and the State, says: "Such is the positive task, embracing at once theory and practice, which the Church undertakes in virtue of the mission, confided to her by Christ, of constructing a Christian society, and, in our own times, of resisting unto victory the attacks of communism. It is the duty of the Christian State to concur actively in this spiritual enterprise of the Church, aiding her with the means at its command, which although they be external devices, have nonetheless for their prime objective the good of souls."[45]

The State-protection over the Church, claimed in the foregoing principle, is, however, purely ministerial and, therefore, does not empower the State to exercise true jurisdiction over her. The Church remains in full liberty in the fulfillment of her mission.[46]

The negative obligation of the State: After having studied what the State must do in favor of the Church, it is equally necessary to consider what the former must not do in its relations to the latter, Leo XIII, says: [The duty of the State is] "neither to organize nor to enact any measure that may compromise its safety." The main reason why this obligation is imposed on the State is the absolute necessity of pursuing the eternal happiness of man. The attainment of man's last end, which is the principal mission of the Church, must not be impeded even in the case in which something unfavorable or detrimental is to be undergone by the civil society.[47]

There are many evident testimonies in the Holy Scripture which can be alleged to prove man's strict obligation to contrive to attain the unchangeable good of heaven, and, if necessary, even

---

[45] Pius XI, Encyclical, *"Divini Redemptoris"* (March 31, 1937)—*AAS*, XXIX, 103. Translation from Koenig, *op. cit.*, n. 1257.

[46] Ottaviani *op. cit.*, II, n. 312.

[47] Cavagnis, *op. cit.*, n. 395.

in detriment to the temporal life. "So if thy right eye is an occasion of sin to thee, pluck it out and cast it from thee; for it is better for thee that one of thy members should perish than that thy whole body should be thrown into hell."[48] "For what does it profit a man, if he gain the whole world, but suffer the loss of his soul? or what will a man give in exchange for his soul?"[49]

In order that the Church may not be impeded by the State in her mission, the civil rulers must see to it that: 1) the civil legislation does not contradict the ecclesiastical laws, because, otherwise, the achievement of man's last end would be rendered difficult, if not impossible all together; for man would not know whom to obey; 2) in case of conflict between the two legislations, the ecclesiastical is permitted to prevail. Thus, if the civil laws hinder the mission of the Church, the latter is empowered not only authoritatively to declare that the citizens are under no moral obligation to obey the State, but also to coerce with due punishment the rulers to change or reform the laws of the State.[50] The following is a wise principle for the state-legislation: "Incipit legislatio civilis ubi desinit ius canonicum."[51]

It must not be thought that the Church is so absorbed in the care of souls as to be unconcerned with those things which pertain to man's temporal and earthly interest. That the Church cooperate with the State in the advancement of temporal prosperity is evidenced in various fields of life:

1) In international life—The Church, in teaching brotherhood among men, establishes a solid basis for international peace and welfare. This brotherhood is based on the common fatherhood of God. Only upon this basis a durable international peace is attainable.

Since war is the direct enemy of unity and peace, the Church has always done her best to prevent this catastrophe among peoples. Taking our present days as an example in this matter, we see that the Church has not spared any effort to avert war from humanity. "Aware of the excesses to which the way is

---

[48] St. Matth., V, 29.
[49] St. Matth., XVI, 26, 27.
[50] Ottaviani, *op. cit.*, II, n. 309.
[51] Cavagnis, *op. cit.*, n. 403.

opened and an impulse provided by a policy which takes no account of God's law, we used every endeavor when war threatened, to avert the supreme catastrophe and to persuade those in power, upon whose shoulders rested the heavy responsibility of decision, to withdraw from an armed conflict and to spare the world a tragedy beyond all foreseeing."[52]

Even when generous efforts fail to produce the desired result, the Church does not desist from benefiting nations. "It remained for us . . . to use every possible endeavor meanwhile to alleviate the misfortunes arising out of the war, endeavors which are not a little obstructed by the impossibility, not yet overcome, of bringing the aid of Christian charity to the regions where the need of it is more urgently felt."[53]

2) In national life—Through the influence of the Church, Christ has willed that priceless benefits should accrue to the earthly prosperity of every nation. St. Augustine gives us an idea of the efficient cooperation of the Church with the State when he addresses the Church in the following terms: "Thou joinest together, not in society only, but in a sort of brotherhood, citizens with citizen, nation with nation, and the whole race of men, by reminding them of their common parentage. Thou teachest kings to look to the interest of their people, and dost admonish the people to be submissive to their kings. With all care dost thou teach all to whom honor is due, and affection, and reverence, and fear, consolation, and admonition and exhortation, and discipline, and reproach, and punishment. Thou showest that all these are not equally incumbent on all, but that charity is owing to all, and wrong-doing to none."[54]

3) In economic life—The Church's mission is also intimately concerned with the economic well-being of its members. The Encyclical Letters of the Popes, v.g., "*Rerum novarum,*" and

---

[52] Pius XII, "*In Questo Giorno di Santa*" Allocution to the College of Cardinals, December 24, 1939)—*AAS,* XXXI, 708, 709. Translation from Koenig, *op. cit.,* n. 1495.

[53] Pius XII, *ibid.* Translation from Koenig, *op. cit.,* n. 1496.

[54] St. Augustine, *De Moribus Ecclesiae Catholicae et de Moribus Manichaeorum* (388) (Migne, *Patrologia Latina*), XXXII, n. 63. Translation from Wynne, *op. cit.,* p. 118.

"Quadragesimo anno," are an evident proof of this.[55] "The nature of our ministry," Leo XIII says, "requires that we be always prompt and ready to bring aid wherever the afflicted cry for comfort, the weak for protection, or the sorrowful for the lifting of their burdens."[56]

Undoubtedly the Pope on this occasion refers to that fact in which "a small number of very rich men have been able to lay upon the teeming masses of the laboring poor a yoke which is little better than slavery itself."[57] Against this powerful dominion of the few over the masses the Church claims justice and charity in behalf of the propertyless and wage-earners. "There is a dictate of nature more imperious and more ancient than any bargain between man and man, that the remuneration must be enough to support the wage-earners in reasonable and frugal comfort. If through necessity for fear of a worse evil, the work-men accept harder conditions because an employer or contractor will give them no better, they are the victims of force and injustice."[58]

"We may lay it down as a general and perpetual law, that working-men's association should be organized and governed as to furnish the best and most suitable means for attaining what is aimed at; that is to say, for helping each individual member to better his condition to utmost in body, mind and property."[59]

Pius XI adds to this the following: "Every effort must, therefore, be made that fathers of families receive a wage sufficient to meet adequately ordinary domestic needs. If in the present state of society this is not always feasible social justice demands that reforms be introduced without delay which will guarantee every adult working man just such a wage."[60]

---

[55] Leo XIII, Encyclical, *"Rerum novarum"* (May 23, 1891)—*ASS*, XXIII, 641-670. Pius XI, Encyclical, *"Quadragesimo anno"* (May 15, 1931), *AAS*, XXIII, 177-228.

[56] Leo XIII, Littera, *"Nihil Nobis"* (August 6, 1893)—*ASS*, XXVI, 74. Translation by the writer.

[57] Leo XIII, Encyclical, *"Rerum novarum"* (May 23, 1891)—*ASS*, XXIII, 642. Translation from Wynne, *op. cit.*, p. 209.

[58] Leo XIII, *ibid.*, p. 662. Translation from Wynne, *op. cit.*, p. 236.

[59] Leo XIII, *ibid.*, p. 667. Translation from Wynne, *op. cit.*, p. 243.

[60] Pius XI, Encyclical, *"Quadragesimo anno"* (May 15, 1931)—*ASS*, XXIII, 200. Translation from *Five Great Encyclicals* (New York: The Paulist Press, 1939), p. 145.

4) In culture and knowledge—The Church fully realizes that human happiness does not consist merely in material prosperity, but principally in the advancement of civilization. It was the Church which saved the libraries, the literatures and the cultural monuments of antiquity from destruction; it fostered every kind of learning, whether sacred or profane, founded universities and schools, inspired and encouraged fine arts in all their noblest manifestations.[61]

Furthermore it was the Church which led humanity from the darkness of paganism and barbarism to civilization. "And in truth, wherever the Church has set her foot, she has straightway changed the face of things, and has attempered the moral tone of the people with a new civilization, and with virtues before unknown. All nations which have yielded to her sway have become eminent for their culture, their sense of justice, and the glory of their deeds."[62]

ARTICLE VI. SIXTH PRINCIPLE

> To exclude the Church, founded by God himself, from the business of life, from the power of making law, from the training of youth, from domestic society, is a grave and fatal error.[63]

This proposition, in other words, means that the State should not be separated from the Church; the union of the two powers is, hereby, advocated. The principle of union of Church and State is a hard saying, especially in our days, even to Catholics. The opposite doctrine, however, is expressly condemned by the Church.[64]

Those who maintain the need for the separation of the two powers can be classified into two groups: 1) Those who assert

[61] Leo XIII, Encyclical, *"Inscrutabili Dei"* (April 21, 1878)—*ASS*, X, 586, 588.

[62] Leo XIII, Encyclical, *"Immortale Dei"* (November 1, 1885)—*ASS*, XVIII, 161. Translation from Wynne, *op. cit.*, p. 107.

[63] Leo XIII, Encyclical, *"Immortale Dei"* (November 1, 1885)—*ASS*, XVIII, 172. Translation from Wynne, *op. cit.*, p. 124.

[64] Pius IX, *Syllabus*, prop., 60. Cf. Denzinger-Bannwart, n. 1755.

that the State is the only society on earth, which by its own nature is perfect; that it is the origin and the main source of all rights. According to this theory the State must be absolutely separated from the Church. "Many wish the State to be separated from the Church wholly and entirely, so that regard to every right of human society, in institutions, customs, and laws, the offices of State, and the education of youth, they would pay no more regard to the Church than if she did not exist; and, at most, would allow all the citizens individually to attend to their religion in private if so minded."[65]

2) Those who theoretically approve the union of the Church and the State, but deny, for the sake of prudence, according to them, its application in practice. "Those who, while they do not approve the separation of Church and State, think nevertheless that the Church ought to adapt herself to the times and conform to what is required by the modern system of government."[66] This theory *"per se"* is false, for it implies that the doctrine of the Church and its very nature are essentially changeable;[67] nevertheless, the censure given by the Church, condemning the separation of the two powers, cannot simply be applied to the second theory, because this theory *"per accidens"* is admissible, that is, there are especial circumstances in which the separation of the two powers may be even advisable. "Such an opinion is sound, if it is to be understood of some equitable adjustments consistent with truth and justice; in so far, namely, that the Church, in the hope of some great good, may show herself indulgent, and may conform to the times in so far as her sacred office permits."[68]

Before proceeding to the reasons why the Church and the State should be in constant concord, it is necessary to study the real and essential meaning of the said principle: *"UNION OF*

---

[65] Leo XIII, Encyclical, *"Libertas Praestantissimum"* (June 20, 1888)—*ASS,* XX, 611. Translation from Wynne, *op. cit.,* p. 160.

[66] Leo XIII, Encyclical, *"Libertas Praestantissimum"* (June 20, 1888)—*ASS,* XX, 612. Translation from Wynne, *op. cit.,* p. 160.

[67] Cappello, *Summa Iuris Publici Ecclesiastici,* n. 290.

[68] Leo XIII, Encyclical, *"Libertas Praestantissimum"* (June 20, 1888)—*ASS,* XX, 612. Translation from Wynne, *op. cit.,* p. 161.

CHURCH AND STATE." Its real meaning can be formulated in the following terms: "The State should officially recognize the Catholic religion as the religion of the Commonwealth; it should recognize and sanction the laws of the Church; and it should protect the rights of the Church, and the religious as well as the other rights of the Church's members."[69]

It does not, therefore, precisely consist, as many falsely think, in that the State should necessarily support the clergy, or that the State should nominate the dignitaries of the Church, fostering thereby numberless abuses greatly pernicious to the welfare of the Church; neither does it consist in that union of State and Church which existed in the Middle age. Pohle (1852-1922) says: "The intimate connection of both powers during the *Middle age* was only a passing and temporary phenomenon, arising neither from the essential nature of the State nor from that of the Church."[70] Hence, the principle of "*UNION OF CHURCH AND STATE*" is not bound up to "any particular form of union that has actually been in operation."[71]

The arguments against the separation of the two powers are: 1) The separation of Church and State is contrary to man's nature; man is absolutely and intrinsically one. His activity, being also essentially one, can by no means be divided so that he could tend at the same time and with the same activity to objectives contradictory one to another. But, if the two powers are separated, the State could easily, and in many instances it really does, prescribe something which is openly contrary to the teaching of the Church. Man would not know whom to obey. Therefore, the separation of Church and State of both of which societies man is a member is contrary to his very nature.[72]

2) The separation of the two powers is an open violation of the obligation of the State, first, towards God, and, secondly, towards the citizens themselves. The first, because in the separation of Church and State religion is considered as some-

---

[69] Ryan and Boland, *op. cit.*, p. 316.
[70] The Catholic Encyclopedia, "Toleration."
[71] Ryan and Boland, *ibid.*
[72] Cappello, *op. cit.*, n. 282.

thing outside the scope of the State, when it should be its very foundation. The State is bound to worship God to whom it owes its being. "For it cannot be doubted but that, by the will of God, men are united in civil society; whether its component parts be considered or its form, which implies authority; the object of its existence; or the abundance of the vast services which it renders to man. Wherefore civil society must acknowledge God as its Founder and Parent, and must obey and reverence His power and authority. Justice, therefore, forbids, and reason itself forbids the State to be godless; . . . ."[73]

The second, because it is the duty of the State to give to the citizens the best opportunity and example to strive earnestly for their last end. This, however, cannot be expected when the State shows disregard to what the citizens highly respect and estimate. "For public authority exists for the welfare of those whom it governs; yet, in so doing, it ought not to diminish, but rather to increase, man's capability of attaining to the supreme good in which his everlasting happiness consists which can never be attained if religion be disregarded."[74]

3) The separation of the two powers is, above all, pernicious to the State itself. "For it is undeniable that harmony between the civil and religious society is most necessary for the tranquility of public order, the foundation of well-being in every sense."[75]

"Religion, of its essence, is wonderfully helpful to the State. For, since it derives the prime origin of all power directly from God himself, with grave authority it charges rulers to be mindful of their duty, to govern without injustice or severity, to rule their people kindly and with almost paternal charity; it admonishes subjects to be obedient to lawful authority, as to the ministers of God; and it binds them to their rulers, not merely by obedience, but by reverence and affection, forbidding all seditions and ven-

---

[73] Leo XIII, Encyclical, *"Libertas Praestantissimum"* (June 20, 1888)—*ASS*, XX, 604. Translation from Wynne, *op. cit.*, p. 150.

[74] Leo XIII, Encyclical, *"Libertas Praestantissimum"* (June 20, 1885)—*ASS*, XX, 605. Translation from Wynne, *op. cit.*, p. 151.

[75] Benedict XV, Allocution, *"In hac quidem"* (November 23, 1921)—*AAS*, XIII, 521-524. Translation from Koenig, *op. cit.*, n. 725.

turesome enterprise calculated to disturb public order and tranquility, and cause greater restrictions to be put upon the liberty of the people."[76]

4) Lastly, the separation of Church and State is greatly injurious to the Church; because in agreement with this principle "the Church is allowed a standing in civil society equal only, or inferior, to societies alien from it; no regard is paid to the laws of the Church, and she who, by the order and commission of Jesus Christ, has the duty of teaching all nations, finds herself forbidden to take any part in the instruction of the people."[77]

Therefore, it is "clear that the two powers, though dissimilar in functions and unequal in degree, ought nevertheless to live in concord, by harmony in their action and the faithful discharge of their respective duties."[78]

---

[76] Leo XIII, Encyclical, *"Libertas Praestantissimum"* (June 20, 1888)—*ASS,* XX, 605. Translation from Wynne, *op. cit.,* p. 151.

[77] Leo XIII, Encyclical, *"Immortale Dei"* (November 1, 1885)—*ASS,* XVIII, 170, 171. Translation from Wynne, *op. cit.,* p. 121.

[78] Leo XIII, Encyclical, *"Libertas Praestantissimum"* (June 20, 1888)—*ASS,* XX, 605. Translation from Wynne, *op. cit.,* pp. 159, 160.

PART TWO

Actuation of the Principles of the Christian Constitution of States in the Philippine Constitution

INTRODUCTION. BRIEF HISTORY OF THE PHILIPPINE CONSTITUTION (1935)

In 1934 the Philippine legislature, by authorization of the United States Congress, called for the election of delegates from all over the country for the purpose of drafting a constitution for the Philippine Commonwealth. "The Philippines is, hereby, authorized to provide for the election of delegates to a Constitutional Convention, which shall meet in the Hall of the House of Representatives . . . not later than October 1, 1934, to formulate and draft a constitution for the government of the Commonwealth of the Philippines, subject to the conditions and qualifications prescribed in this Act. . . ."[1]

In accordance with the said provision of the Tydings-McDuffie Law, 202 delegates were chosen by direct vote of the people in July 10, 1934 to form the Constitutional Convention. And on February 19, 1935 the fundamental law of the new Commonwealth was successfully formulated and signed by all the delegates except one, and for its ratification by the people a plebiscite was held on May 14 of the same year.[2]

The character of the Philippine Constitution is similar to that of many modern Republics. As a matter of fact the members of the Constitutional Convention had taken as sources for it the Malolos Constitution,[3] the American constitution, Spain's republican constitution, the Mexican constitution, and the constitutions of some South American nations.[4]

---

[1] *Tydings-McDuffie Law,* sec. I (Statutes of the United States of America passed at the second session of the Seventy-third Congress, 1934, pp. 456-465. Cf. Villarruz, N. V., *Commentaries and Opinions on the Constitution of the Philippines* (Manila, 1935), Appendix A.

[2] Cf. Villarruz, *op. cit.,* Preface, p. vii.

[3] This was the political Constitution of the Philippine Republic created after the war against Spain. Cf. Kalaw, Maximo M., *Development of Philippine Politics,* Appendix D, p. 430.

[4] Alip, M. Eufronio, "The Making of our Constitution," cf. *Unitas* (1938), XVI, 403. (*Unitas* is the organ of the Faculty of the University of St. Thomas.)

There is nothing, therefore, essentially new in this constitution, except the adaptation of the foreign laws to the particular needs and customs of the Philippines. Wenceslao Vinzons, however, one of the delegates, objected during the discussions on the Constitution as a whole; "That it failed to reflect the tradition, history, political training, racial character of the Filipinos . . . and that it adopted a system of government copied from Latin American Republics which have had the sad experience of being unsuccessful in their government."[5]

The present constitution which was particularly promulgated for the Commonwealth will continue to be the basic law of the Philippines upon the complete withdrawal of the American sovereignty.[6] The jurisdiction of the constitution covers "all the territory ceded to the United States by the treaty of peace concluded between the United States and Spain on the 10th day of December, 1898, the boundaries of which are set forth in Article III of said treaty, together with those islands embraced in the treaty between Spain and the United States concluded at Washington on the 7th day of November, 1900."[7]

---

[5] *Unitas* (1938), XVI, 402.

[6] Philippine Constitution (1935), Art. XVII.

[7] *Tydings-McDuffie Law,* sec. I, cf. Villarruz, *op. cit.,* Appendix A.

CHAPTER IX

The Philippine Constitution

ARTICLE I. THE AIM OF THE CONSTITUTION

It is a principle in Christian philosophy that the State is established for the common good, and, therefore, must be concerned with all in general, and also, whenever it is possible, with the individual interests of the citizens.

This primary objective of the civil society—the common good of the nation—is specifically described in the Preamble to the Constitution of the Philippines. "The Filipino People, imploring the aid of Divine Providence, in order to establish a government that shall embody their ideals, conserve and develop the patrimony of the nation, promote the general welfare, and secure to themselves and their posterity the blessings of independence under the regime of justice, liberty, and democracy, do ordain and promulgate this Constitution."[1]

Unlike many other constitutions, the Philippine Constitution, besides enunciating in a comprehensive way the main objective of the Commonwealth, specifies in details the means by which to attain the general welfare of the nation:

I) By the conservation and development of the national patrimony—National patrimony comprises both the spiritual and material possessions of the country. The ideals, the customs and the traditions of the race, as well as the man-power supplied by the individual constituents of the Filipino nation constitute the spiritual patrimony. Article XII of the Constitution provides for the conservation and utilization of the natural resources of the country.[2]

---

[1] Philippine Constitution (1935), *Preamble.*

[2] Constitution of the Philippines (1935). This article has six sections: sec. I—deals with the nationalization of the natural resources; sec. 2—the disposal of public agricultural lands; sec. 3—the extent of private agricultural lands; sec. 4—the expropriation of private lands; sec. 5—the prohibition of alien landholdings; sec. 6—government in business.

For the conservation and advancement of the national spiritual heritage several provisions are embodied in the Constitution. It provides the establishment and maintenance of a complete and adequate system of public education; free public primary instruction; the establishment of schools with the "aim to develop moral character, personal discipline, civic conscience, and vocational efficiency, and to teach the duties of citizenship"; the creation of scholarship in arts, science, and letters for specially gifted citizens.[3]

II) By the attainment of the blessings of independence under the regime of justice, liberty, and democracy. To this effect, the Constitution guarantees to every citizen the protection of his civil and political rights;[4] insures justice to every one who demands

---

[3] Philippine Constitution (1935), art. XIII, sec. 4 and sec. 5.

[4] Philippine Constitution (1935), art. III (Bill of Rights)

Sec. I (1) "No person shall be deprived of life, liberty, or property without due process of law, nor shall be denied the equal protection of the laws."

(2) "Private property shall not be taken for public use without just compensation."

(3) "The right of the people to be secure in their persons, houses, papers, and effects against unreasonable searches and seizures shall not be violated, and no warrants shall issue but upon probable cause, to be determined by the judge after examination under oath or affirmation of the complainant and the witnesses he may produce, and particularly describing the place to be searched, and the persons or things to be seized."

(4) "The liberty of abode and of changing the same within the limits prescribed by the law shall not be impaired."

(5) "The privacy of communication and correspondence shall be inviolable except upon lawful order of the court or when public safety and order require otherwise."

(6) "The right to form associations or societies for purposes not contrary to law shall not be abridged."

(7) "No law shall be made respecting an establishment of religion, or prohibiting the free exercise thereof, and the free exercise and enjoyment of religious profession and worship, without discrimination or preference, shall forever be allowed. No religious test shall be required for the exercise of civil or political rights."

(8) "No law shall be passed abridging the freedom of speech, or of the press, or the right of the people peaceably to assemble and petition the government for redress of grievances."

(9) "No law granting a title of nobility shall be enacted, and no person holding any office of profit or trust shall, without the consent of the National

it;[5] establishes the merit system for the distribution of the civil services;[6] articles VI, sec., 8, n. 1, 2, and VII, sec., 12, n. 2, provide both legislative and executive inhibitions respectively to avoid any possible abuse by the government officials in the administration of justice to the people.

III) By the promotion of social justice—"The promotion of social justice to ensure the well-being and economic security of all the people should be the concern of the State."[7] "Only by

---

Assembly, accept any present, emolument, office, or title of any kind whatever from any state."

(10) "No law impairing the obligation of contracts shall be passed."

(11) "No ex post facto law of bill of attainder shall be enacted."

(12) "No person shall be imprisoned for debt or nonpayment of poll tax."

(13) "No involuntary servitude in any form shall exist except as a punishment for crime whereof the party shall have been duly convicted."

(14) "The privilege of the writ of habeas corpus shall not be suspended except in cases of invasion, insurrection, or rebellion, when the public safety requires it, in any of which events the same may be suspended wherever during such period the necessity for such suspension shall exist."

(15) "No person shall be held to answer for a criminal offense without due process of law."

(16) "All persons shall before conviction be bailable by sufficient sureties, except those charged with capital offenses when evidence of guilt is strong. Excessive bail shall not be required."

(17) "In all criminal prosecutions the accused shall be presumed to be innocent until the contrary is proved, and shall enjoy the right to be heard by himself and counsel, to be informed of the nature and cause of the accusation against him, to have a speedy and public trial, to meet the witnesses face to face, and to have compulsory process to secure the attendance of witnesses in his behalf."

(18) "No person shall be compelled to be a witness against himself."

(19) "Excessive fines shall not be imposed, nor cruel and unusual punishment inflicted."

(20) "No person shall be twice put in jeopardy of punishment for the same offense. If an act is punished by a law and an ordinance, conviction or acquittal under either shall constitute a bar to another prosecution for the same act."

(21) "Free access to the courts shall not be denied to any person by reason of poverty."

[5] Philippine Constitution (1935), art. VIII, Sections 1, 2, 3, 4, 5, 6, 7, 8, 9, 10, 11, 12, and 13.

[6] Philippine Constitution (1935), art. XI, sec. 1.

[7] Philippine Constitution (1935), art. II, sec. 5.

making it economically secure can a modern government have independence, wield influence in the world, preserve law, order and justice."[8]

"This fundamental principle of social justice recognized in the Constitution is more beneficial to the laboring class than to any other class of people in the Philippine Islands."[9]

IV) By the maintenance of peace—"The Philippines renounces war as an instrument of national policy, and adopts the generally accepted privileges of international laws as a part of the law of the nation."[10]

This spirit of peace adopted by the Constitution has been repeatedly and publicly stressed by the chief executive. President Quezon says: "Our Constitution, as will be seen, is inspired in the spirit of the most intense nationalism. But thank God, it is a nationalism of the sort that recognizes that law and justice should rule the world, as every nation is but a member of the large human family. This is the purport of Section 3, Article II of the Constitution. In the light of this ordinance, the spirit of nationalism which pervades our Constitution should be read, and when the time comes for us to knock at the door of the council of nations, its members cannot but welcome us as a peace-loving and righteous people."[11]

On another occasion President Quezon stated: "The fact that in this constitution you have given the Philippine Commonwealth and the Philippine Republic all the powers that it needs in order to have an efficient national defense and thus be able to meet the eventualities of the future must not be thwarted to mean that we are imbued with ideals except of those of peace, good-will and friendship. For you have in your Constitution solemnly declared that it is the national policy of our people to renounce war as an instrument of national policy."[12]

---

[8] Lim, National Economic Protectionism under Constitution,—*Saturday Herald,* Manila, May 18, 1935.

[9] Camus, How Constitution Protects Filipino Laborers,—*Saturday Herald,* Manila, April 27, 1935.

[10] Philippine Constitution (1935), art. II, sec. 3.

[11] Quezon, Convention Speech, February 12, 1935. Cf. Villarruz, *op. cit.,* p. 10.

[12] Quezon, Baccalaureate address before the Constitutional Convention, February 5, 1935. Cf. Villarruz, *op. cit.,* p. 11.

In the opinion of the author, the Philippine Constitution, regarding its objective and the means to attain that end, is in conformity with the principles of the Christian Constitution of States, with the exception of certain provisions which deal with religion. These, however, will properly be considered in another part of this work.

ARTICLE II. FORM OF GOVERNMENT AND ORIGIN OF SOVEREIGNTY

a) Form of Government—The Tydings-McDuffie Independence Law, in one of its mandatory provisions, ordained that the Constitution of the Philippines should be republican in form.[13] This was not, however, the only reason which led the Framers of the Constitution to the adoption of a democratic institution, but also their very training and experience in the art and science of self-government. The lesson and experience which they had during the American regime would give them no other choice except a republican government.[14]

Thus the Constitutional Convention unanimously approved the insertion of the following provision in the Declaration of Principles: "The Philippines is a republican State. Sovereignty resides in the people and all government authority emanates from them."[15] This provision is just a "reaffirmation by the Convention of its faith in republican institutions and in the ultimate wisdom of the rule of the people, preferring a democratic government to an aristocratic, oligarchical, autocratic, or monarchical government."[16]

The conception of a republican State which the members of the Constitutional Convention had is the generally accepted one among the modern democratic nations. Due, however, to the great influence of American Constitutional law in the Philippines, often-times it is necessary to go to American sources when dealing

---

[13] *Tydings-McDuffie Law,* sec. 2 (a). Cf. Aruego, José, *The Framing of the Philippine Constitution* (2 vols., Manila, 1937), Appendix F.

[14] Villarruz, *Commentaries and Opinions on the Constitution of the Philippines,* p. 7.

[15] The Philippine Constitution (1935), Art. II, sec. 1.

[16] Aruego, *op. cit.,* I, 132.

with the interpretation of the Philippine Constitutional law; many questions thereof "must be looked at from the same angle here [in the Philippines] as in the United States."[17]

James Madison, in respect to the conception of a republican State, says: "We may define a republic to be a government which derives all its powers directly or indirectly from the great body of the people; and is administered by persons holding their offices during pleasure, for a limited period, or during good behavior. It is essential to such a government that it be derived from the great body of the society, not from an inconsiderable proportion, or a favored class of it. It is sufficient for such a government that the persons administering it be appointed either directly or indirectly, by the people; and that they hold their appointments by either of the tenures just specified."[18]

It is the avowed doctrine of the Church concerning the constitution and government of a State, as it has been already expounded, that the several existing forms of government are all capable of insuring the general welfare of nations, if wisely and justly managed. The Church, therefore, does not prohibit the people from selecting the form of government they like best.

b) Origin of Sovereignty—The Philippine Constitution expressly states that "sovereignty resides in the people and all government authority emanates from them."[19] According to this constitutional provision the government derives its power to rule from the people; the people, therefore, constitute the fountainhead of all governmental authority. This same doctrine was also emphasized in the Independence Law, according to whose tenor the Constitution was required to be drafted, i.e., that the government should receive its power from the governed.[20]

The officers of the government, according to this principle of the Constitution, are but representatives of the people, exercising the authority delegated to them, agents and not masters of the

[17] Malcolm and Laurel, *The Constitutional Law of the Philippines* (3. ed., Manila, 1936), p. 44.

[18] Cf. Aruego, *op. cit.*, I, 132.

[19] Strictly speaking the Philippines, during the Commonwealth period, is not a sovereign nation, because it is still dependent of the United States pending the final and complete withdrawal of the sovereignty thereof.

[20] Malcolm and Laurel, *op. cit.*, p. 88.

nation. "Consequently they could not, nor should they be permitted to be more powerful than the people."[21]

Does this mean to say that the supreme authority in the Philippines, which the government exercises, derives from the people without any reference to God? In all the discussions made on this subject during the Convention, there was no specific mention about the ultimate source of sovereignty. Nevertheless, the answer to the above question can be deduced from the very Christian spirit with which the Constitutional Convention was conducted and the Constitution itself is animated. As a matter of fact the Convention was opened with a solemn invocation by a Catholic Bishop, His Excellency Alfredo Versoza of the Diocese of Lipa, Batangas, P. I. The President of the Convention, Delegate Claro Recto, in his valedictory address at the adoption of the final drafting of the Constitution, repeated a part of the invocative prayer acknowledging that God is the source of all powers: "I am confident that they [the future generations] will judge it [the Constitution] recognizing the nobility of our purposes and the magnitude of our efforts . . . our desire to realize for our people, through this Constitution, that noble eagerness of purpose vibrant in these words of human wisdom and divine fervor with which an illustrious Prelate, pride of the native clergy, invoked the blessings of the Supreme Creator on the memorable day of our inauguration. 'Father, thou art the Fountain-head of all power and the source of all happiness, make of the Philippines a nation of happy people within thy Kingdom.' "[22]

Also the Preamble to the Constitution leads us to the same answer. "The Filipino people, imploring the aid of the Divine Providence, in order to establish a government that shall embody their ideals . . ." [recognizes with full faith and confidence the Supreme Legislator, and, therefore, believe that the fountain of all authority is God]. This is but natural to the Filipino people, because they have been long imbued with Christian virtues and principles which have naturally become a part of their nature and national institutions. "In the true Christian

[21] Aruego, *op. cit.*, II, 715.

[22] Cf. Aruego, *op. cit.*, II, 693.

spirit," says President Quezon, "the Filipino people have laid down the foundation stone of their independent existence. When they drafted the Constitution for the Commonwealth which is also to be the Constitution of the Philippine Republic, they sought first the guidance of the Divine Providence. . . ."[23]

Finally in the inauguration of the Commonwealth, His Excellency Gabriel Reyes, the Catholic Archbishop of Cebu, P. I. pronounced this solemn invocation in which God is expressly acknowledged as the Giver of all power.

"To the King of ages, Immortal, Invisible, the only God, be honor and glory for ever and ever, Amen."

"We pray Thee, O God of Wisdom and Justice, from Whom all authority comes, to assist with thy light and power the authorities who have been elected by the will of their brethren . . . the President and the *Vice-Preisent*. . . ."[24]

Conclusion—It is undoubtedly evident that the Philippine Constitution holds that the multitude is the repository of the supreme authority in the State; that the government derives its power directly from the Filipino people, who in turn have received it from the Almighty.

Although the Church has not pointed out definitively her doctrine concerning whether supreme authority descends directly or not upon the rulers, yet, due to the risk of public disturbance and seditions easily occasioned by the flattering phrases, that the people are sovereign, that the government officials are but agents and that they are, by no means, more powerful than the people governed, the theory which teaches that God confers directly the supreme power upon the persons chosen by the people to rule, in the writer's opinion, insures more permanently the stability of the nation itself. The thought that the government officials receive the authority to rule directly from God, once they are chosen by the people, inspires in those who govern the sacred responsibility of discharging diligently the duties they have towards God and the people for whose welfare they are in power, and makes the people more prompt to obey the laws of the government.

---

[23] Messages of the President (5 vols., Manila Bureau of Printing, 1938), III, part I, 93, 94.

[24] Aruego, *op. cit.*, II, 727, 728.

CHAPTER X

State and Religion

ARTICLE I. STATE-RELIGION

The Filipinos, liberty-loving people, whose gigantic struggles for freedom are recorded in every page of their history, have embodied a Bill of Rights in the Constitution of the Philippine Commonwealth. This Bill of Rights is not an invention of theirs, but a reproduction of the provisions contained in the principal legislation passed by the United States Congress for the administration of civil affairs in the Philippines.[1]

The Tydings-McDuffie Independence Law also provided for the inclusion of a Bill of Rights; but even without this mandatory provision the members of the Constitutional Convention would have adopted such a Declaration of Rights. It was their conviction that "there is no Constitution, worthy of the name, without a Bill or Declaration of Rights. This Bill of Rights is to be, as it were, the living gospel of the liberties of the people. It is not to be a catalogue or compilation of inhibitions or restrictions upon the people, because the people are sovereign. Rather, it is to be the palladium of their liberties and immunities, so that their persons, their homes, their peace, their livelihood, their happiness and their freedom may be safe and secure from an ambitious ruler, and envious neighbor, or a grasping State."[2]

There had been an attempt to formulate the Bill of Rights on the basis of social rights, i.e., on the fact that the State is, in the modern theory, the creator and dispenser of all rights; but fortunately this atheistic conception of the State was rejected. Delegate Laurel, in opposition to this proposal, said: "We should not,

[1] Bustos and Fajardo, *New Philippines* (Manila, 1934), contains "The President McKinley's Instruction to the Taft Commission," p. 465; "The Philippine Bill of Rights," p. 473; "The Jones Law," p. 499.

[2] Laurel, Speech delivered before the Constitutional Convention on the Bill of Rights,—cf. Aruego, *op. cit.*, II, 1060, 1061.

however, be allured by the new and untried dogmas and theories in the formulation of our Bill of Rights, and again I suggest that we adopt a conservative attitude in this connection. Again it were better that we keep close to the shores; let others venture on the deep."[3] The Bill of Rights of the Philippine Constitution is based, as that of the Federal Constitution of the United States, on the inherent and natural rights of man.

Among the constitutional rights guaranteed in the Magna Charta of the Philippine Commonwealth, there are some which have a definite relation with public ecclesiastical law.

I) Religious Liberty—The Constitution provides: "No law shall be made respecting an establishment of religion, or prohibiting the free exercise thereof, and the free exercise and enjoyment of religious profession and worship, without discrimination or preference, shall forever be allowed."[4] This provision was literally taken from the Jones Law, and was readily approved and incorporated in the Constitution. The reason for its inclusion was that "no system of liberty is complete which does not guarantee religious freedom."[5]

It is to be noticed that the basic principles regulating the separation of Church and State in the United States and the free exercise of religion have been fully adopted in the Philippines. And in accordance with these principles the State must: 1) not profess any religion; 2) equalize all religions.

I) The Philippine government does not profess any religion. When the International Eucharistic Congress took place in the City of Manila in 1937, the President of the Philippines, His Excellency Manuel L. Quezon, requested that all references to the Government of the Commonwealth should be eliminated from the program of the Congress, fearing that such references would be misunderstood and would be interpreted as an official participation of the State in that religious ceremony. To this effect the President wrote thus to the Archbishop of Manila: "I hope I am a good Catholic. As such, in my individual capacity, there is nothing that I should not be glad to do to give added solemnity to the celebration of the Eucharistic Congress . . . but, as President of

---

[3] Laurel, *ibid.;* cf. Aruego, *op. cit.,* p. 1061.

[4] The Constitution of the Philippines (1935), art. III, sec. 1 (I).

[5] Laurel, *ibid.;* cf. Aruego, *op. cit.,* p. 1045.

the Philippines I am not in a position to do what your program calls for."[6]

On another occasion the President expressly stated this indifference of the government towards religion. "As an individual, I worship my God in accordance with my own religious belief— But as the head of the State I can have no more to do with the Catholic Church than I can with the Protestant denominations, the Aglipayans, the Mohammedans or any other religious organizations or sects in the Philippines."[7]

From all the foregoing it can be concluded without any fear of mistake that the Philippine Constitution is permeated with the spirit and philosophy of religious indifferentism. The description laid down by Leo XIII about States based upon similar principles fits exactly the Philippine government. The Pope says: ". . . It believes that it is not obligated to make public profession of any religion; or to inquire which of the very many religions is the only true one; or to prefer one religion to all the rest; or to show to any form of religion special favor; but, on the contrary, is bound to grant equal rights to every creed, so that public order may not be disturbed by any particular form of religious belief." [It believes] "that all questions that concern religion are to be referred to private judgment; that everyone is free to follow whatever religion he prefers, or none at all if he disapprove of all."[8]

This attitude of the Philippine government proceeds from the false principle that the State as such is not bound by any kind of duty towards the Creator. There is no reason why the State, i.e., the officials of the government as such, should be indifferent and offer no homage to God by making public profession of religion, when the State, as any other individual, owes its being to the Almighty; it is by the Divine will that the civil society exists. Men are bound to worship God, not only as individuals, but also as organized in society.[9]

[6] Messages of the President (Quezon), II, part I, p. 274.

[7] Messages of the President (Quezon), II, part I, pp. 126, 127.

[8] Leo XIII, Encyclical, *"Immortale Dei"* (November 1, 1885)—*ASS*, XVIII, 170. Translation from Wynne, *The Great Encyclical Letters of Pope Leo XIII*, p. 121.

[9] Leo XIII, *ibid.*, p. 163. Translation from *ibid.*, p. 110.

Moreover, the State as such is bound to worship God by public profession of the true religion, especially in a Catholic country, because of the great benefits which derive from religion itself. Temporal peace and tranquility which are the greatest and most efficient factors in fostering public welfare can not be attained without true morality, i.e., without obedience to the laws of the government and respect for the rights of others. This obligation, which binds in conscience, would not be efficacious without the full knowledge that God is one's Creator and Judge; all this, however, is what religion teaches and inculcates.[10]

As a matter of fact the Philippine government acknowledges these benefits. "The Catholic Church," says President Quezon, "stands for law and order, for respect and obedience to constituted authority, for public and private morality, for human brotherhood, and its influence in this regard will be helpful to our country, especially at this time."[11]

Finally, the State should be concerned with religion, because "those who are in authority owe it to the Commonwealth not only to provide for its external well-being and the conveniences of life, but still more to consult the welfare of men's souls in the wisdom of their legislation. And, what is still more important . . . although the civil authority has not the same proximate end as the spiritual, or proceeds on the same line, nevertheless in the exercise of their separate powers they must occasionally meet."[12]

The Philippine Constitution in its provision based on State-indifference towards religion, that the government as such must not profess any religion, is contrary to the teaching of Christian philosophy; moreover, it is contrary to the traditions and history of the country which for more than three hundred years had made public profession of the Catholic religion.

This neutrality towards religion is, however, not absolute. The government believes in the existence of God and, therefore, can not in practice avoid taking a positive and favorable attitude toward religion, as it will be seen in later consideration on this subject.

---

[10] Cavagnis, *Institutiones Iuris Publici Ecclesiastici*, n. 433.

[11] Messages of the President (Quezon), II, part I, p. 127.

[12] Leo XIII, Encyclical, "*Libertas Praestantissimum*" (June 20, 1888)—*ASS*, XX, 603. Translation from Wynne, *op. cit.*, p. 148.

ARTICLE II. RELIGIOUS EQUALITY

The Philippine Constitution, based on the principle that every man is free to profess as he may choose any religion or none, necessarily presupposes, as all followers of religious indifferentism do, that there can be no certainty which, among the many existing religious denominations, is the true one; that there is no one who can authoritatively and competently show to the people which is the true religion. From such a principle follows the necessity to guarantee freedom of worship and to equalize all religions before the law.

"The Constitution of the Philippines establishes religious tolerance and religious equality."[18] There is every indication that tolerance is not understood here in its real sense, but is taken in the sense of liberty of conscience, i.e., that everyone is given equal rights and liberty in all that pertains to the profession, propagation and exercise of one's proper religion; and consequently, that no law shall be passed preferring one religion to all the rest, or showing to any form of religion special favor, but that the State is bound to grant equal rights to all religions.

Tolerance in its genuine meaning is the act of allowing, for the sake of avoiding worse, the existence of beliefs and religious practices differing from one's own. In the case of a State, tolerance would imply first, that the State professes its own religion; secondly, that, only for the sake of public order and tranquility it permits, with some unwillingness, the existence of other religious denominations. The Philippine Constitution, however, does not provide for this kind of tolerance, but full equalization of religions or pure liberty of conscience. It is not tolerance, because the Philippine government as such does not profess any religion of its own, and, therefore, willingly grants equal rights to both truth and error in matters of religion.

All religions are welcome in the Philippines as all of them are considered by the government beneficial to itself and to the people. President Quezon in a speech on the separation of the Church and the State stated: "Lastly I want to say that the

---

[18] Malcolm and Laurel, *The Constitutional Law of the Philippines*, c. XXIII, p. 419.

Catholic Church and every church in fact can be and should be of great help to the Government and the people of the Philippines."[14]

The assumption that all forms of religion are equal is contrary to reason itself. According to the principle of contradiction, two contradictory propositions can not both be true. As a matter of fact, one denomination's creed is often-times the denial of the other; the Mohammedans consider Christ as a prophet like Mohammed; the Catholics adore Christ as God, and consider Mohammed as a deceiver; the Jews, on the other hand, killed Christ as a public sinner and, thus, still expect the Messias. When the government, therefore, gives equal rights and privileges to these contradictory religious denominations, it openly equalizes error with truth which is one only and cannot contradict itself. The government in doing so practically declares to the people that there is nothing certain in matters of worship, and, consequently, leads them to despise all religions, even the true one, as mutually contradictory.

"To hold therefore that there is no difference in matters of religion between forms that are unlike each other, and even contrary to each other, most clearly leads in the end to the rejection of all religion in both theory and practice. And this is the same thing as atheism, however it may differ from it in name. Men who really believe in the existence of God must, in order to be consistent with themselves and to avoid absurd conclusions, understand that differing modes of divine worships involving dissimilarity and conflict even on most important points, cannot be equally probable, equally good, and equally acceptable to God."[15]

Above all, equalization of religions implicitly denies, or at least, pretends to ignore the positively-revealed doctrine of God, that "the only-begotten Son of God established on earth a society which is called the Church, and to it He handed over the exalted and divine office which He had received from His Father, to be continued through the ages to come. 'As the Father hath sent me, I also send you. Behold I am with you all days, even to the consummation of the world.' "[16]

---

[14] Messages of the President (Quezon), II, part I, p. 127.

[15] Leo XIII, Encyclical, "*Immortale Dei*" (November 1, 1885)—*ASS*, XVIII, 172. Translation from Wynne, *op. cit.*, p. 123.

[16] Leo XIII, *ibid.*, p. 164. Translation, *ibid.*, p. 112.

The equalization of the Catholic Church in the Philippines with all the religious denominations is, in my opinion, unfair to it. This appears evident even if the matter is considered only in the light of history and undeniable facts. An American author on Philippine history says: "The part which the Roman Catholic Church has played in the life of the Filipino people for nearly four hundred years has given that institution a position in the Philippines which is not artificial, but which reaches into the very roots of society and is different from that which any church occupies in the United States."[17]

The Catholic Church side by side with the Spanish Empire christianized the Filipino people, imparting to them the civilization and the customs of which they are at present justly proud, and for which they are considered the only Christian country in the Far East. The role which the Catholic Church plays in the educational system is a distinctive contribution to the intellectual life of the nation. It has now 280 schools of all grades from kindergarten to university, with almost 100,000 students.[18] One of the glories of the Philippines in the educational field is the Pontifical University of Sto. Tomas, the first university of its kind in the whole Orient. It was established in 1611; twenty-five years before the oldest university of the United States was founded. Within its halls many of the past and present scholars, and the majority of the government officials have made their studies.[19] "By the grace of God, the Filipino people are disciples of our Lord Jesus Christ. Theirs is a Christian civilization. Most of their scholars, for more than three hundred and fifty years, have drunk from the fountains of wisdom which finds its source from the *Summa Theologica* of St. Thomas Aquinas, as taught in another university, the University of Sto. Tomas, in Manila, the oldest university under the American Flag—my own Alma Mater."[20]

The great majority of the population are members of the Catholic Church, i.e., 12,603,365 of the total population which is

---

[17] Hayden, *The Philippines,* p. 560.

[18] Hayden, *op. cit.,* p. 553.

[19] *Ibid.,* p. 554.

[20] Messages of the President (Quezon), II, part I, pp. 93, 94.

16,000,303.[21] The Catholic Church began in the Philippines with their discovery and is now established all over the country, whereas the Aglipayans who constitute the Filipino schism came into existence only in 1901; Protestantism was introduced into the Islands only after the American occupation; the Moros or the Mohammedans are the Filipinos who occupy mostly the Island of Mindanao which is still relatively unexplored; the Pagans are those living in the forests and the mountainous section of the country; the Shintoists are the Japanese population; the Buddhists are the Chinese and probably a very limited number of the Japanese.[22] These religions, due to their recent foundation or to their very limited number of followers in the Philippines, have hardly contributed to the progress and development of the nation, and yet, they are given the same equal rights and privileges before the government as the Catholic Church, the religion of the great majority and the greatest benefactress of the Philippines since their discovery.[23]

It is not hard to find the true religion established by God, especially in a Catholic country as the Philippines, "if only it be sought with an earnest and unbiased mind; for proofs are abundant and striking . . . the fulfillment of prophecies; miracles in great number; the rapid spread of the faith in the midst of enemies and in face of overwhelming obstacles; the witness of the martyrs, and the like. From all these it is evident that the only true religion is the one established by Jesus Christ Himself, and which He committed to His Church to protect and to propagate."[24]

ARTICLE III. RELIGIOUS TOLERANCE

There are circumstances, especially in our modern days, in which religious tolerance can be permitted even in a Catholic nation. "The Church, indeed, deems it unlawful to place the

[21] Cf. Census of the Philippines (1939), Vol. II, c. VIII, p. 381.

[22] Hayden, *op. cit.*, pp. 570-571.

[23] Hayden, *op. cit.*, p. 553. The Protestant schools are fewer than the Catholic in number and have relatively smaller enrollment.

[24] Leo XIII, Encyclical, "*Immortale Dei*" (1885)—*ASS*, XVIII, 164. Translation from *The Great Encyclical Letters of Leo XIII*, pp. 111-112.

various forms of divine worship on the same footing as the true religion, but does not, on that account, condemn those rulers who, for the sake of securing some great good or hindering some great evil, allow patiently custom or usage to be a kind of sanction for each kind of religion having its place in the State."[25]

The principal reason which justifies the tolerance of false worship is the attainment of greater good and the avoidance of greater evil. "But, to judge aright, we must acknowledge that the more a State is driven to tolerate evil the further is it from perfection; and that the tolerance of evil which is dictated by political prudence should be strictly confined to the limits which its justifying cause, the public welfare, requires. Wherefore, if such tolerance would be injurious to the public welfare, and entail greater evils on the State, it would not be lawful; for in such a case the motive of good is wanting. And although in the extraordinary condition of these times the Church usually acquiesces in certain modern liberties, not because she prefers them in themselves, but because she judges it expedient to permit them, she should in happier times exercise her own liberty; and, by persuasion, exhortation, and entreaty, would endeavor, as she is bound, to fulfill the duty assigned to her by God of providing for the eternal salvation of mankind. One thing, however, remains always true—that liberty which is claimed for all to do all things is not, . . . of itself desirable, inasmuch as it is contrary to reason that error and truth should have equal rights."[26]

The public welfare would be endangered by religious intolerance if it is morally impossible for the State to deny political toleration to dissenting sects without causing public seditions. This usually happens in countries in which several religious denominations have taken root and are firmly established therein in virtue of a fact historically accomplished.[27] According to Pohle: "If religious freedom has been accepted and sworn to as a fundamental law in a Constitution, the obligation to show

[25] Leo XIII, *ibid.*, p. 174. Translation, *ibid.*, p. 127. Encyclical, *"Libertas Praestantissimum"* (1888)—*ASS,* XX, 609. Translation, *ibid.*, p. 157.

[26] Leo XIII, Encyclical, *"Libertas Praestantissimum"* (June 20, 1888)—*ASS,* XX (1888), 610. Translation from Wynne, *op. cit.*, p. 158.

[27] Ottaviani, *op. cit.*, II, 68. Moulart, *L'Eglise et L'Etat* (4. ed., Paris, 1895), p. 317.

this tolerance is binding in conscience."[28] On the basis of the foregoing reasons religious tolerance in its real sense would be, in my belief, permissible in the Philippines, i.e., if the Philippine government would acknowledge the Catholic religion as the State-religion, and tolerate the rest. First, a provision which guarantees religious liberty has been sworn to in virtue of the Constitution. To disregard this provision would be the violation of oaths and loyalty. Secondly, to hamper and proscribe the free exercise of the religious activities of established religious congregations in the Islands could hardly be done without violent public convulsions. Finally, it is morally impossible for the government to depart from the universally accepted principle of modern States, religious tolerance. These arguments would not have had the same force forty years ago when the Philippines were ceded to the United States.[29]

ARTICLE IV. RELIGIOUS FREEDOM

The Church, the ever solicitous guardian of human liberty, considers religious freedom as an inherent and inalienable right of man, "the highest of natural endowment."[30] This assertion would certainly be a surprise to those who continually accuse the Church of being hostile to human liberty.[31] Since religious freedom is an equivocal phrase, it is necessary to distinguish the genuine sense from the false one. Religious freedom, if taken in the sense that man is completely free to worship God in any form of religion he chooses or not at all, is, as it has been repeatedly asserted, false. The true and genuine meaning of religious freedom is clearly set forth by His Holiness Pius XII in his Christmas message to the whole world. "Religious freedom," he says, "is the right to the worship of God in private and public and to carry on religious works of charity."[32] This free-

[28] *The Catholic Encyclopedia,* "Toleration."

[29] Hayden, J., *The Philippines* (Macmillan, N. Y., 1942), p. 560.

[30] Leo XIII, Encyclical, "*Libertas Praestantissimum*" (1888), *ibid.,* p. 593.

[31] *Ibid.,* p. 600.

[32] Pius XII, Christmas Message to the Whole World (December 24, 1942). Translation from Koenig, *Principles for Peace,* n. 1846.

dom, although it is a personal privilege of man, nevertheless, is not exclusively attributed to him, but also to other legal or moral entities, the Church and the State. Accordingly, man has the right to be free and be protected in his private and public worship of God; the State has the right to be free in the fulfillment of its "obligation to protect the rights of all the citizens, regardless of their individual belief, as long as it does not turn to anarchy under religious pretext . . ."; the Church too has the right to "enlighten men in the true way of worship without applying compulsion or force, and to be free in the fulfillment of this supernatural and natural task from outside interference, be it directed against the Church as such, or against her faithful members; . . . ."[33]

The ecclesiastical legislation on this matter is entirely animated with the spirit of freedom, v.g., the Church does not admit any adult to the regenerating waters of baptism without his free consent.[34] The Church, it is true, is accused of being intolerant, in that she prohibits her members from participating in the services of other denominations, and thus violate the principle of freedom of worship. But to Catholics and to any one who considers without bias this attitude of the Church it appears evident that it is by no means contrary to freedom of worship. The Church, as the States do, enacts proper laws by which to lead its members to the attainment of the common good. Thus, one of its laws is the prohibition to take part in the religious functions of other denominations outside the Catholic Church which, according to her doctrine, are false. "No society at all, neither Church nor State can exist without its laws being obeyed by its members."[35] As no citizen is free to choose which laws to obey and which not, thus no Catholic is free to obey or not the laws of the Church. Human liberty needs to be safeguarded by law,

---

[33] Ploechl, "Fundamental Principles of Philosophy of Canon Law"—The *Jurist* (A Quarterly Review: The Catholic University of America), IV, n. 1 (1944), 93.

[34] Canon 752 I. "Adultus, nisi sciens et volens probeque instructus, ne baptizetur; . . .": Canon 745, § 2, 2°.

[35] Ploechl, *ibid.*, p. 92.

"for law is the guide of man's actions; it turns him towards good by its rewards, and deters him from evil by its punishment."[36]

The Constitution of the Philippine Commonwealth expressly guarantees religious freedom according to the Church's view. "No law shall be made respecting an establishment of religion, or prohibiting the free exercise thereof, and the free exercise and enjoyment of religious profession and worship, without discrimination or preference, shall forever be allowed."[37]

ARTICLE V. LIBERTY OF CONSCIENCE

The principle *"liberty of conscience"* carries with itself under the appearance of truth and justice the spirit of atheism.[38] If physical liberty is meant by it, then liberty of conscience is perfectly reasonable and justified. "And in fact the Church is wont to take earnest heed that no one shall be forced to embrace the Catholic faith against his will for, as St. Augustine wisely reminds us, 'man cannot believe otherwise than of his own will.' "[39] If moral liberty, however, is meant by liberty of conscience; then it is legitimate only if it is taken "to mean that man in the State may follow the will of God and, from a consciousness of duty and free from every obstacle, obey His commands. This indeed, is true liberty, a liberty worthy of the sons of God, which nobly maintains the dignity of man, and is stronger than all violence or wrong—a liberty which the Church has always desired and held most dear."[40] But liberty of conscience is entirely false, if it is taken in the sense that the mind is free to adhere to falsehood and the will to choose and follow what is wrong; to worship God or not at all. When such liberty is "offered to man, the power is given him to pervert or abandon with impunity the most sacred of duties and to exchange the unchangeable good

[36] Leo XIII, Encyclical, *"Libertas Praestantissimum"* (June 20, 1888)—*ASS,* XX (1888), 597. Translation from Wynne, *op. cit.,* p. 140.

[37] The Constitution of the Philippines (1935), art. III, sec. 1 (7).

[38] Ottaviani, *op. cit.,* II, n. 268.

[39] Leo XIII, Encyclical, *"Immortale Dei"* (November 1, 1885)—*ASS,* XVIII (1885), 175. Translation from Wynne, *op. cit.,* p. 127.

[40] Leo XIII, Encyclical, *"Libertas Praestantissimum"* (June 20, 1888)—*ASS,* XX (1888), 608. Translation from Wynne, *op. cit.,* pp. 155, 156.

for evil; which . . . is no liberty, but its degradation, and the abject submission of the soul to sin."[41]

The Church, therefore, willingly approves whatsoever is good in the principle of *"Liberty of Conscience,"* but strongly condemns whatsoever evil it contains. "We are," says Pius XI, "happy and proud to wage the good fight for the liberty of conscience, not indeed . . . for the liberty of conscience which is an equivocal expression too often distorted to mean the absolute independence of conscience, which is absurd in a soul created and redeemed by God. . . ."[42]

That the Philippine Constitution guarantees the liberty of conscience can be logically deduced from the fact that it grants liberty of speech and of the press which are the principal manifestations of the said principle.[43] And in the opinion of the writer, this liberty of conscience granted by the Constitution is understood according to the atheistic view, i.e., every citizen is free to worship God or not at all.

ARTICLE VI. FREEDOM OF SPEECH AND PRESS

The Committee on the Bill of Rights submitted to the Convention the provision of the Jones Law on freedom of speech and of the press.[44] At the insistence, however, of Delegate Recto, President of the Convention, an attempt was made during the discussions on this subject to modify the provision pertaining to freedom of the press with the following: "There shall be no limitations to the freedom of the press except those required by good morals and public order. No publication shall be suspended except by final decision of a competent court."[45]

---

[41] Leo XIII, Encyclical, *"Libertas Praestantissimum"* (June 20, 1888)—*ASS,* XX (1888), 604. Translation from Wynne, *op. cit.,* p. 150.

[42] Pius XI, Encyclical, *"Non abbiamo bisogno"* (June 29, 1931)—*AAS,* XXIII (July 6, 1931), 283. Translation from Koenig, *Principles for Peace,* n. 1051.

[43] Ottaviani, *op. cit.,* II, 57.

[44] Jones Law, sec. 3—"No law shall be passed abridging the freedom of speech, or of the press, or the right of the people peaceably to assemble and petition the Government for redress of grievances."

[45] Aruego, *The Framing of the Philippine Constitution,* I, 165.

A strong opposition against this proposed modification was voiced particularly by the Press. The *Philippine Herald* thus published: "As far as the first sentence goes, no possible objection could be raised but the second sentence gives room for very grave doubts. By stating that no publication shall be suspended the implication is that a publication may be suspended. There is thus a serious threat against the freedom of written expression in this country and that is more than we have expected this Constitutional Convention to do. The courts would be given an arbitrary power they have not heretofore exercised, for not only would they be made to pass judgment on cases of libel but also order a publication to stop.

It is realized that there are publications that corrupt morals, and that there are sheets run by irresponsible individuals bent on poisoning the public mind. But we believe that, if a constitutional precept preventing such morbid tendencies of man is a necessity, the continued existence of the responsible Press need not be endangered by a sweeping generalization."[46]

Laurel, chairman of the Committee on the Bill of Rights, vigorously opposed the modification. "It should be observed that the limitations mentioned with respect to freedom of the press are all well-known and sanctioned under the existing provision of the United States Constitution. A careful analysis of the proposed change will show that it is not an improvement to the provision contained in the Jones Law. Upon the other hand let us not create the impression that the freedom of the speech is more important than the freedom of the press. Why restrict or liberalize the one and not the other when both are equally important? The limitations as to 'good morals' should better be left out. We cannot define them in the Constitution even if we should want to. Also, the suppression of a given publication by a final order of a competent court is an unwarranted limitation upon the freedom of the press, and is ineffective at that, because pending final judgment of the court, the publication may continue. I, therefore, plead for the acceptance of the original recommendation of the Committee on Bill of Rights. . . ."[47]

---

[46] *The Philippine Herald,* Editorial (Manila, P. I., November 20, 1934). Cf. Aruego, *op. cit.,* I, 166.

[47] Laurel, Speech before the Convention. Cf. Aruego, *The Framing of the Philippine Constitution,* II, 1058, Appendix J.

The members of the Convention evidently were convinced by the arguments of both Laurel and the Press, since the original provision, as it appears in the Jones Law, was finally incorporated in the Constitution. "No law shall be passed abridging the freedom of speech, or of the press, or the right of the people peaceably to assemble and petition the Government for redress of grievances."[48] This liberty guaranteed in the Philippine Constitution is not license, but is "liberty regulated by the law."[49] In virtue of this constitutional right every citizen can publish the truth with good motives and for justified ends without previous censorship. It does not, however, grant an absolute right to the citizens to say and publish whatever they please.[50]

Malcolm and Laurel cite the concept of Apolinario Mabini, one of the outstanding statesmen of the country, on liberty. "Many believe that if they have liberty they have complete freedom to do the bad and good alike. Liberty is freedom to do right and never wrong; it is ever guided by reason and the upright and honorable conscience of the individual. The robber is not free, but is the slave of his own passions, and when we put him in prison we punish him precisely because he is unwilling to use true freedom. Liberty does not mean that we shall obey nobody, but commands us to obey those whom we have put in power and acknowledge as the most fit to guide us, since in this way we obey our own reason."[51] The right to freedom of speech and of the press is a moral power and as such it was not given to man that he should use it "indifferently to truth and falsehood, to justice and injustice."[52]

The Church does not deny that "men have a right freely and prudently to propagate throughout the State what things soever are true and honorable, so that as many as possible may possess them; but lying opinions, than which no mental plague is greater, and vices which corrupt the heart and moral life, should be

---

[48] The Constitution of the Philippines (1935), art. III, sec. 1 (8).

[49] Malcolm and Laurel, *The Constitutional Law of the Philippines,* p. 311.

[50] Laurel, Speech before the Convention—cf. Aruego, *The Framing of the Philippine Constitution,* II, p. 1059, Appendix J.

[51] Cf. Malcolm and Laurel, *op. cit.,* p. 312.

[52] Leo XIII, Encyclical, *"Libertas Praestantissimum"* (June 20, 1888)—*ASS,* XX, 605. Translation from Wynne, *op. cit.,* p. 152.

diligently repressed by public authority, less they insidiously work the ruin of the State."[53] In matters that are certain and evident there can be no such freedom of speech and of the press; man is necessarily bound to assent to what is certainly and evidently true. The intellect is ordained by its own nature to adhere to goodness and truth, which in turn "cannot be changed at option. These remain ever one and the same, and are no less unchangeable than nature itself."[54]

"In regard, however, to all matters of opinion which God leaves to man's free discussion, full liberty of thought and of speech is naturally within the right of every one; for such liberty never leads men to suppress the truth, but often to discover it and make it known."[55]

Freedom of speech and of the press as understood in the Constitution of the Philippines is not equal to unbridled license to say and print anything. "The enjoyment of a private reputation is as much constitutional right as the possession of life, liberty, or property. So the constitutional provisions do not permit the publication of libelous, blasphemous, or indecent articles, or other publications injurious to public morals or private reputation."[56]

The purpose of the freedom of speech and of the press in a nation must be the welfare of the people. "The interest of society and the maintenance of good government demand a full discussion of public affairs. The public acts of public men may lawfully be made the subject of comment and criticism. Their fitness for office may be discussed, and their acts, character, and motives may be challenged."[57] "Complete liberty to comment on the conduct of public men is a scalpel in the case of free speech. The sharp incision of its probe relieves the abscesses

---

[53] Leo XIII, Encyclical, *"Libertas Praestantissimum," loc. cit.;* translation from *ibid.*, p. 152.

[54] Leo XIII, Encyclical, *"Immortale Dei"* (November 1, 1885)—*ASS,* XVIII, 172. Translation from Wynne, *op. cit.*, p. 124. Cavagnis, *op. cit.*, n. 511.

[55] Leo XIII, Encyclical, *"Libertas Praestantissimum," loc. cit.*, p. 606. Translation from Wynne, *op. cit.*, p. 152.

[56] Wercester v. Ocampo (1912) 22 Phil. 42. Cf. Malcolm and Laurel, *op. cit.*, pp. 398-399.

[57] Malcolm and Laurel, *op. cit.*, p. 399.

of officialdom. Men in public life may suffer under a hostile and an unjust accusation; the wound can be assuaged with the balm of a clean conscience."[58]

"Men have the right to attack, rightly or wrongly, the policy of a public official, with every argument good or bad, which ability can find and ingenuity invent. They may show, by argument good or bad, such policy to be injurious to the individual and to society. They may demonstrate, by logic true or false, that it is destructive of human freedom, and will result in the overthrow of the nation itself. But the law does not permit men falsely to impeach the motives. . . . Men may argue, but they may not traduce. Men may differ, but they may not, for that reason, falsely charge dishonesty. Men may look at policies from different points of view, and see them in different lights, but they may not, on that account, falsely charge criminality, immorality, lack of virtue, bad motives, evil intentions, or corrupt heart or mind. Men may falsely charge that policies are bad, but they cannot falsely charge that men are bad."[59]

The concept and purpose which the Framers of the Constitution had, in the drafting of this provision, on the freedom of speech and of the press, are, in my opinion, theorically unquestionable. Furthermore, the commentaries and some decisions made by the Supreme Court on the true interpretation of such liberties clearly manifest the genuine sense of liberty as understood in the constitutional guarantee.

Since, however, this freedom of speech and of the press is an equivocal expression, having in itself a true and a false sense, there is a constant danger that citizens especially liberals would, under the pretext of such liberties, foster doctrines which are openly against the intention of the Fathers of the Bill of Rights. As a matter of fact when in 1937 the Municipal Board of Manila sought to pass a statute prohibiting public conferences on birth-control as a doctrine that was suicidal to national life and that was evidently against morals, some of the members of the Board protested that the suppression of such conferences was a violation of the right to freedom of speech and assembly. Mr. Ben-

[58] U. S. v. Bustos (1918) 37 Phil. 731: cf. Malcolm and Laurel, *op. cit.*, p. 399.

[59] U. S. v. Contreras (1912) .23 Phil. 513-513: cf. Malcolm and Laurel, *op. cit.*, p. 401.

jamin Alderman Atienza thus argued: "Is this a free country . . .? Since the time of Galileo, official intolerance, ignorance, and bigotry have been stumbling block to progress in science and civilization."

"We do not have to take sides on the birth-control issue. But we have to defend the right of every individual, in a free, democratic country like ours and give constitutional guarantee to every citizen of the freedom of speech and of assembly."

"Authorities on constitutional law are inclined to treat these fundamental rights in almost the same way: that they are of superior importance and no measure can be adopted to restrict them. So it was held that no injunction can lie against a newspaper to prevent publication of a particular item, on the claim that the latter is libelous. It was also held that a peaceful meeting could not be prevented on the ground that seditious doctrines were to be preached therein. If violations of law are noted after publication, or after the holding of the meeting, the guilty parties may be prosecuted. But the law cannot *'a priori'* conclude that there would be such a violation before violation in such matters is committed and prevent the exercise of the freedom of the press, speech and assembly."[60]

It would not be necessary to show the fallacy of this argumentation; it is sufficiently demonstrated through this example how easily these liberal expressions lead to false interpretation of true liberty and thus become the fountain-head of manifold erroneous doctrine. The Church condemns only that liberty of speech and of the press which surpasses moderation and passes beyond the bounds and end of true liberty.[61]

ARTICLE VII. ACADEMIC FREEDOM

The Constitution provides: "Universities established by the State shall enjoy academic freedom."[62] This provision was

[60] Cf. *The Sunday Tribune* (Manila, P. I., August 8, 1937), "Is this a free Country?" p. 10.

[61] Leo XIII, Encyclical, *"Libertas Praestantissimum"* (June 20, 1888)—*ASS*, XX, 605.

[62] The Constitution of the Philippines, art. III, sec. 5. This constitutional guarantee is not found in the Bill of Rights; due, however, to its close relation to the liberties embodied therein it will be briefly considered in this chapter.

unanimously approved by the members of the Convention without any objection.[63]

The main purpose of this guarantee is, in the first place, to free the State's universities from any political interference and, in the second place, to safeguard the intellectual freedom of the professors in the investigation of truth, in the discussions of vital problems and in the manifestation of their conclusions both by speech or by press.[64] Professors of state universities enjoy this academic freedom in all branches of science. "Under this provision we would never have a repetition of that famous case in which a Tennessee University Professor was prosecuted criminally for explaining to his pupils the Darwinian Theory of Evolution."[65]

"This is a precept in our Constitution," says President Quezon, "that is noteworthy, for a university, to be a real temple of learning and scholarship, must constantly be in quest of truth, and in that quest it must be unhampered in its thought and expression. Unless our scholars are thus protected, it will be difficult for them to accomplish their task, of pursuing truth relentlessly to advance the frontiers of science and learning."[66] That there is a latent possibility of danger in this unlimited liberty of State universities was acknowledged by the Philippine Press. "Academic freedom could thus be a source of danger; but disciplining atmosphere in the university itself would be made extant following an abuse of academic freedom. Furthermore, there will be a natural inhibition in the exercise of this grant of right. Intellectual integrity will make many desist from a vocal expression of attitude and reaction, because intellectual integrity warns them they may be unhappy in their rationale. A legal grant, academic freedom becomes those who have the capacities of mind and character to transform it into a social asset."[67]

---

[63] Aruego, *op. cit.*, vol. II, p. 630.

[64] *Loc. cit.;* cf. Villarruz, *Commentaries and Opinions on the Constitution of the Philippines*, p. 120.

[65] Lim, a letter on Academic Freedom of Universities, cited by Villarruz, *op. cit.*, p. 120.

[66] Quezon, Convocation Speech at the University of the Philippines (Feb. 12, 1935)—cf. Villarruz, *op. cit.*, p. 120.

[67] *The Sunday Tribune* (Manila, September 1, 1935), Editorial.

No other restraint or control is imposed on university professors than university discipline, state supervision, and intellectual integrity. Experience testifies that this exorbitant liberty enjoyed in all branches of science by universities, without the necessary restraint of laws imposed by the Church and reason, easily degenerates into license. Many extravagant and mad theories have been asserted by university professors who enjoyed this prerogative, despite their intellectual integrity and instinct for truth. Gillis[68] gives the following writers with their respective assertions: Cosmo Hamilton, in a debate with G. K. Chesterton, speaking on marriage said: "Marriage is not made in heaven, but on the top of a tram, or in a canoe on a placid stream or during a walk in the woods, when the boy says 'Will you marry me?' and the girl answers 'I will.' That is the marriage, any demand that it be recorded in a magistrate's office or at a city hall or in a church is tyranny. Metchnikoff in his explanation on the nature of man said: "Man is a kind of miscarriage of the ape." And Nietzsche asserted that: "Morality is the greatest enemy of life." A thousand other assertions like these could be cited.

In such unrestricted liberty, the Church sees, as in all other modern liberties, the easy transition from true liberty into license. Thus academic freedom "in order that it may deserve the name must be kept within limits, lest the office of teaching be turned with impunity into an instrument of corruption."[69] The Church teaches that there are two kinds of truth, the natural and the supernatural. "Of natural truth" [which are the only concern of state universities], "such as the principles of nature and whatever is derived from them immediately by our reason, there is a kind of common patrimony in the human race. On this, as a firm basis, morality, justice, religion, and the very bonds of human society rest: to allow people to go unharmed who violate or destroy it, would be most injurious, most foolish, and most inhuman."[70]

---

[68] *The Church and Modern Thought* (Washington, D. C., 1935), p. 43.

[69] Leo XIII, Encyclical, *"Libertas Praestantissimum"* (June 20, 1888)—*ASS*, XX, 606. Translation from Wynne, *op. cit.*, p. 153.

[70] Leo XIII, Encyclical, *"Libertas Praestantissimum," loc. cit.*, p. 606. Translation from Wynne, *op. cit.*, p. 153.

Since the truth of divine revelation and that of nature are one, deriving from the same fountain, God, although in a different way and since they consequently cannot contradict one another, the Church rejects as necessarily false any doctrine concerning natural science that is at variance with the divinely revealed truth. In doing this the Church is by no means constituted, as often times asserted by enemies, a stumbling block to science and civilization, but, on the contrary, its doctrine, "so far from being an obstacle to the pursuit of learning and the progress of science, or in any way retarding the advance of civilization, in reality brings to them the sure guide of shining light. There is no reason, therefore, why genuine liberty should grow indignant, or true science feel aggrieved, at having to bear the just and necessary restraint of laws by which, in the judgment of the Church and of reason itself, human teaching has to be controlled."[71]

While the Church imposes the necessary restraint on branches of learning which have necessary connection with faith and morals, it leaves an open and vast field "to man's industry and genius, containing all those things which have no necessary connection with Christian faith and morals, or as to which the Church exercising no authority, leaves the judgment of the learned free and unconstrained."[72]

---

[71] Leo XIII, Encyclical, *"Libertas Praestantissimum"* (June 20, 1888)—*ASS*, XX, 607. Translation from Wynne, *op. cit.*, pp. 154, 155.

[72] Leo XIII, Encyclical, *"Libertas Praestantissimum"* (June 20, 1888)—*ASS*, XX, 608. Translation from Wynne, *op. cit.*, p. 155.

CHAPTER XI

ATTITUDES OF THE STATE TOWARDS RELIGION IN PRACTICE

The neutrality of the Philippine government towards religion is, however, not absolute; there are several provisions in the very Constitution which clearly indicate the deep concern of the government with religion, although the State in theory refrains from any formal acceptance of it.

The proofs of this friendly policy of the State towards religion are: 1) Invocation of Divine Assistance. Besides the invocation of divine assistance which was made at the opening of the Constitutional Convention and at the inauguration of the Commonwealth, one finds a similar petition in the Preamble to the Constitution which implores the guidance and aid of Divine Providence for a prosperous and successful government of the country.

2) Chaplain's Service.[1] President Quezon emphatically states the necessity of religion for the armed forces when he says: "I am very much interested in the organization of a Chaplain's service, not only because the National Defense Act so authorizes, but also because I am deeply convinced that religion is a moral force of incalculable value for good, and I am determined to take every precaution that will guarantee to our Army the whole benefits contemplated by the creation of this service."

"Let me avow publicly the firm conviction that faith in God and the practice of one's religious belief keeps a man, perhaps more than any other consideration, within the bounds of law and helps him in the performance of his duties. This is not to say, of course, that an atheist or a man without religion may not be a good citizen. It is, however, true that a people who honestly and intelligently practice that religion which they profess are in little danger of social disorder and disintegration."[2]

---

[1] The Constitution of the Philippines (1935), art. VI, sec. 13, n. 3.

[2] *Messages of the President* (Quezon), 5 vols., Manila: Bureau of Printing, 1938), III, 283.

3) The Exemption from Taxes. "Cemeteries, Churches, and parsonages or convents, appurtenants thereto, and all lands, buildings and improvements used exclusively for religious, charitable or educational purposes shall be exempt from taxation."[3] The residence of the Archbishop (Catholic) of Manila, in accordance with this exemption Statute, was held exempted from taxation by the Supreme Court of the Philippines.[4] The exemption from the land-tax, also, has been applied by a local Court not only to the land actually occupied by the rectory, but likewise to the surrounding ground or garden thereof.[5]

4) Optional Religious Instruction in Public Schools. "Optional instruction shall be maintained in the public schools as now authorized by law."[6] "The optional religious training in public schools is a profession as a people of our faith in God, and that we give due importance to religion without making its teaching compulsory so as to keep inviolate the principle of separation of Church and State."[7]

5) Oath of Office. The Constitution ordains: "Before he enter on the execution of his office, the President shall take the following oath or affirmation: 'I do solemnly swear (or affirm) that I will faithfully and conscientiously fulfill my duties as President of the Philippines, preserve and defend its Constitution, execute its laws, do justice to every man, and consecrate myself to the service of the Nation. So help me God.' "[8]

---

[3] The Constitution of the Philippines (1935), art. VI, sec. 14. This privilege accorded to all religious corporations was enjoyed even before the Constitution; it was in the Administrative Code.

[4] Catholic Church v. Hastings (1906) 5 Phil. 701: cf. Malcolm and Laurel, *The Constitutional Law of the Philippines*, p. 375.

[5] Bishop of Nueva Segovia v. Provincial Board of Illocos Norte (1928) 51 Phil. 352: cf. Malcolm and Laurel, *op. cit.*, p. 357.

[6] The Constitution of the Philippines (1935), art. XIII, sec. 5. Administrative Code of 1917, art. 927, 928. These statutes permit the priest or the minister to teach religion in the public schools for one-half hour three times a week to pupils whose parents or guardians desire it and express it in writing.

[7] Quezon, Convention Speech (February 12, 1935). Cf. Villarruz, *op. cit.*, pp. 119, 120.

[8] The Constitution of the Philippines (1935), art. VII, sec. 3. "In case of affirmation, the last sentence will be omitted."

All that is ordained by the foregoing provisions constitutes, indeed, what public profession of religion means, although it is very insignificant if compared with what is accorded by the principle of union of Church and State. Public profession of religion does not strictly and necessarily require that the State should legally adopt one form of religion; the State can manifest it in several ways, by adoption, support, or mere toleration of religion.[9]

[9] Ryan and Boland, *Catholic Principles of Politics*, p. 313.

CHAPTER XII

Legal Status of the Church in the Philippines

ARTICLE I. SEPARATION OF CHURCH AND STATE

The Philippine Constitution establishes, in regard to its relation to the Catholic Church, the principle of separation of the two powers. "No law shall be made respecting the establishment of religion, or prohibiting the free exercise thereof, and the free exercise and enjoyment of religious profession and worship, without discrimination or preference shall for ever be allowed. No religious test shall be required for the exercise of civil or political rights."[1] "No public money or property shall ever be appropriated, applied, or used directly or indirectly, for the use, benefit, or support of any sect, church, denomination, sectarian institution, or system of religion, or for the use, benefit, or support of any priest, preacher, minister, or other religious teacher or dignitary as such, except when such priest, preacher, minister or dignitary is assigned to the armed forces, or to any penal institution, orphanage, or leprosarium."[2]

This separation of Church and State in the Philippines is understood to be "real, entire, and absolute."[3] "The State has nothing to do with the Church nor the Church with the State," once stated President Quezon and then added: "We should be thankful that there is here this separation of the Church and the State and freedom of worship. The Church itself is better off when entirely disconnected from the Government and the Government in turn when disassociated from the Church."[4]

"The citizens of this country, with a back-ground of trouble and revolution because of the union of the Church and the State

---

[1] The Constitution of the Philippines (1935), art. III, sec. 1 (7).

[2] *Ibid.*, art. VI, sec. 13 (3).

[3] Malcolm and Laurel, *op. cit.*, p. 421.

[4] Messages of the President (Quezon), II, 126, 127.

under the Spanish regime, must feel genuine satisfaction in the re-incorporation of the principle of the Malolos Constitution, of President McKinley's Instruction, and of the Philippine Autonomy Act, with respect to religious freedom. . . ."[5] It is to be observed that these troubles and revolutions were not precisely against the Christian doctrine and civilization, but against its accompanying abuses committed by the friars.[6]

The principal reasons, therefore, which caused the Framers of the Constitution to re-incorporate the principle separation of Church and State in the fundamental law of the country were: first, that the union of the two powers would cause to both the Church and the State more harm than good; second, that the union of the Church and the State under the Spanish regime caused several insular revolutions. These alleged reasons derive from the misconception of the said principle. Many modern politicians confound the union of the two powers with confusion of the two, supposing that it implies that the clergy should meddle in political affairs and the government in the ecclesiastical.[7]

The fact that the union of Church and State during the Spanish regime had caused troubles in the Philippines, as alleged by Osias, by no means makes the principle blameworthy. Taking for granted that it did really cause conflicts at that time, still no reason is provided there for rushing to the general conclusion that the principle of the union of Church and State will inevitably be harmful in the Philippines under all circumstances. As it has been already stated the principle of the union of Church and State is not necessarily bound up with any form of union that has been in actual use, and, therefore, the union of the two powers in the Philippines would not precisely mean the repetition of the sad experience during the Spanish regime. Some South American republics had had the same experience under Spain, and yet, have conserved the union of Church and State in its

---

[5] Osias, The Constitution and the Education,—*Tribune* (Manila, June 4, 1935), cf. Villarruz, *op. cit.*, p. 119.

[6] Eulogio B. Rodriquez, *A Brief Study of the Filipino Struggle for Freedom*—cf. Bustos and Fajardo, *The New Philippines*, p. 20.

[7] Moulart, *L'Eglise et l'Etat* (4. ed., Paris, 1895), p. 269.

essential element, i.e., the State-recognition of the Catholic faith and the sanction of the ecclesiastical laws.[8]

The idea that the Church would be in a better condition when separated from the State and the fear that the ecclesiastical authorities would interfere in merely political affairs are well manifest in the following statement pronounced by Quezon. "It is of the utmost importance to the Church itself, and no less to the State, that the separation of their powers, as well as the independence of one from the other within their respective sphere of action, be held inviolate. I should want it known that the policy of this Government is to follow strictly the letter and spirit of those precepts of the Constitution which prohibit the interference by the State in ecclesiastical matters, and which likewise imply the firm stand of the State in not allowing ecclesiastical authorities in meddling with purely State matters."[9]

This division of jurisdiction into spiritual and temporal is precisely the principle of the Church even when she claims the union of Church and State. That there exist in the principle of union of Church and State the possibility of abuses both on the part of the clergy and of the State-officials and the danger of conflicts between the two powers is, however, sincerely acknowledged.[10]

It should be recalled that the prosperity of the Church does not necessarily follow from the state of separation, for the Church flourishes whenever she is accorded liberty to exercise her mission. Leo XIII, after praising the friendly policy of the United States Government of America towards the Catholic Church and

---

[8] Argentina—La Constitución de 1860, art. II: "El Gobierno Federal sostiene el culto Católico Apostólico Romano." Art. 67, "Corresponde al Congreso . . . conservar el trato pacífico con los indios, y promover la conversión de ellos al Catolicísmo."

Bolivia—La Constitución de 1880, art. II: "El Estado reconoce y sostiene le Religión Católica, Apostólica, Romana, permitiéndo el ejercicio de otro culto."

Colombia—Según el Concordato de 1887, art. 1: "La Religión Católica es la religión del Estado."

Perú—La Constitución de 1860 también establece le Religión Católica como la religión de la nación.

[9] Messages of the President (Quezon), III, 279, 280.

[10] *The Catholic Encyclopedia,* "Toleration."

the marvelous progress thereof, flatly stated, however, that "although all this is true, it would be very erroneous to draw the conclusion that in America is to be sought the type of the most desirable status of the Church, or that it would be universally lawful or expedient for the State and Church to be, as in America, dissevered and divorced. The fact that Catholicity [in America] is in good condition, nay, is even enjoying a prosperous growth, is by all means to be attributed to the fecundity with which God has endowed his Church, in virtue of which unless men or circumstances interfere, she spontaneously expands and propagates herself; but she would bring forth more abundant fruits if, in addition to liberty, she enjoyed the favor of the laws and the patronage of the public authority."[11]

While this is true in the United States, in other nations, as Mexico and Russia, in which the two powers are separated, the Church is not only denied her freedom, but bitterly persecuted.[12]

The theory of separation of Church and State, as doctrinal system or *"per se"* is condemned by the Church; *"per accidens,"* however, under some extraordinary circumstances and for the sake of avoiding greater evil, the separation of the two powers can be tolerated. But even in this case, "an equitable adjustment consistent with justice and truth"[13] should be agreed upon between the Church and the State. This mutual understanding, or a sort of treaty now called concordat, would be consistent with justice and truth only under the following condition, i.e., that the Church be not despoiled of her nature and rights as a perfect society.[14]

[11] Leo XIII, Encyclical, *"Longinqua Oceani"* (January 6, 1895)—*ASS*, XXVII, 390. Translation from Wynne, *op. cit.*, pp. 323, 324.

[12] Mexico—La Constitución de Nov. 18, 1926, establece la separación del Estado de la Iglesia, además esta separación es tál que prácticamente equivale a una directa persecución. Cf. Pius XI, Encyclical, *"Iniquis afflictisque"* XVIII, 467. Russia—Constitution of 1919, art. 4: "Afin d'assurer aux travailleurs une réelle liberté de conscience, l'Eglise est separée de l'Etat, l'école est séparéede l'Eglise et la liberte de propagande religieuse et antirelgieuse est reconnue a tour les citoyens." Cf. Ottaviani, *op. cit.*, II, n. 420.

[13] Leo XIII, Encyclical, *"Libertas Praestantissimum"* (June 20, 1888)—*ASS*, XX, 603.

[14] Cappello, *Summa Iuris Publici Ecclesiastici*, n. 291.

ARTICLE II. JURIDICAL PERSONALITY OF THE CHURCH

Although the Philippine legislation has failed to recognize the Catholic Church as a perfect society, nevertheless, its juridical personality is recognized on an equal basis with the other religious corporations by the following provision: "The right to form associations or societies for purposes not contrary to law shall not be abridged."[15] Philippine jurisprudence and the decisions of the Supreme Court on this matter confirm such juridical personality of the Catholic Church, as having the power to hold, acquire, dispose of its property, to sue and to be sued.[16] It cannot be deprived of its property or liberty without due process of law, much like natural persons, as provided by the process clause of the Constitution itself.[17] Associations duly organized within the Church are also recognized by the State as legally constituted corporations.[18]

Moreover, the Church has, under the protection of the law, the right to create tribunals and to pass final judgment on controverted questions of faith and morals, and ecclesiastical discipline where and when her members are concerned.[19] Decisions of ecclesiastical courts on civil rights which depend upon religious matters are, likewise, recognized by the civil tribunals as settled questions, duly adjudicated by another competent authority.[20]

These privileges of the Church are considered as liberal concessions on the part of the State, because of immemorial usage and custom, and not as rights deriving from her divine institution as a perfect society. Thus Justice Willard in the case of Barlin v. Ramirez said: "The suggestion, that the Catholic Church does not enjoy juridical personality in the Philippines, made with ref-

---

[15] The Constitution of the Philippines (1935), art. III, sec. I (6).

[16] U. S. v. Avila (1918), 38 Phil. Cf. Malcolm and Laurel, *op. cit.*, p. 409. 383.

[17] The Constitution of the Philippines (1935), art. III, sec. I (1), (2).

[18] Malcolm and Laurel, *op. cit.*, p. 409.

[19] *Ibid.*

[20] Verzosa v. Fernandez (1930) 55 Phil. 307; Gonzalez v. Archbishop of Manila (1929), 280 U. S. 1-19, 74 L. ed. 131-138, 50 Sup. Ct. Rep. 5. Cf. Malcolm and Laurel, *op. cit.*, p. 423.

erence to an institution which antedates by almost a thousand years any other personality in Europe, and which existed when Grecian eloquence still flourished in Antioch, and idols were still worshipped in the temple of Mecca, does not require serious consideration."[21]

While, on the one hand, the Church shows itself indulgent and adaptable to the pretended exigencies of our modern times, it does endeavor, on the other, to restore the normal relations between the two powers and strongly claim its rights whenever the opportunity offers itself. This is evidenced in all the Concordats concluded between the Holy See and Christian States, concerning the mutual limits of their respective powers on affairs of common jurisdiction.[22]

---

[21] Cited by Malcolm and Laurel, *op. cit.*, p. 426.

[22] Concordato fra la Santa Sede e L'Italia—*AAS,* XXI (1929), 275, 294: Tratto fra la Santa Sede e L'Italia—*AAS,* XXI (1929), 209, 221: "Il Concordato dell' Il Febbraio instaura un regime di concordia e di collaborazione, non gia di confuzione fra lo Stato e la Chiesa. La concordia e la collaborazione presuppongono tra i due poteri, l'uno dominante nel campo della coscienza religiosa, l'altro nel campo civile e politico. Ma poichè tra i due campi vi sono rapporti e interferenze continui, così la necessità dell' accordo e della collaborazione fra lo Stato e la Chiesa appare manifesta. Tale coordinazione il Concordato disciplina con lo spirito del maggior reciproco rispetto tra le due potestà." Cf. Del Giudice, *Corso di Diritto Ecclesiastico* (Milano: Stab., Tipo-Litografico G. Tenconi—1929-1930), p. 277: Concordat with Romania (1929), *AAS,* XXI, 441, 454: Concordat with Lithuania (September 20, 1927)—*AAS,* XIX (1927), 425, 433.

CHAPTER XIII

Matters of Common Jurisdiction

ARTICLE I. EDUCATIONAL PROVISION

Notwithstanding the principle of separation of Church and State, in virtue of which neither of the two powers has anything to do with the other, limiting their activities within their respective fields of action, the Church strictly within the spiritual and the State within the temporal, yet, because there are vital problems in the nation itself which, due to their twofold aspect, religious and civil, must pertain to the jurisdiction of both, a harmonious interplay of the action of the two powers is unavoidable.

Education and marriage are the common ground on which Church and State have common interest. These are the two most important fields creating problems which involve both religious and social aspects and often-times provoke controversy between Church and State.

Educational Provision—The Constitution clearly acknowledges that parents have the natural right and obligation of imparting to their children the education they need and that the role of the State in this matter is merely subsidiary. "The natural right and duty of parents in the rearing of the youth for civic efficiency should receive the aid and support of the Government."[1]

In the first draft of the Constitution the following provision on public instruction was formulated. "All educational institutions shall be under the supervision and subject to the laws of the State. The Government shall provide at least free public elementary instruction, and citizenship training for the able-bodied adult members of the State. All schools shall aim at inculcating moral character, personal discipline, civic conscience, and vocational efficiency. The duties of citizenship shall be taught in

---

[1] The Constitution of the Philippines (1935), art. III, sec. 4.

the schools. Optional religious instruction in public schools as now authorized by law shall be maintained."[2]

Before its final incorporation into the Constitution, Delegate Araneta proposed the suppression of the phrase "subject to the laws of the State," because, he said, such provision implies the danger that it would be misinterpreted in the future as an absolute control of the State over all schools and such interpretation would be a direct violation of the liberties embodied in the Bill of Rights. Besides, State-supervision over all educational institutions would be more than enough to guarantee the safety of the nation.[3] The proposal was rejected by the members of the Convention, and the original provision was retained.

The Committee on style, however, rephrased the "subject to the laws of the State" into "under the supervision of and subject to regulation by the State," as it now appears in the present Constitution.[4]

The foregoing process of the formation of this provision gives us an idea of its real spirit and intention. Although it does not provide that the State has absolute control over all schools, it empowers the government to prescribe by law a set of conditions under which all educational institutions shall be organized. "All colleges in the Philippines," says President Quezon in a speech at San Juan de Letran, "are now, under the Constitution, subject to supervision by the State. No college can obtain government recognition unless it abides by the mandates of the Constitution.

---

[2] Aruego, *The Framing of the Philippine Constitution,* II, 614.

[3] Aruego, *op. cit.,* II, 616.

[4] The Constitution of the Philippines (1935), art. XIII, sec. 5. "All educational institutions shall be under the supervision of and subject to regulation by the State. The Government shall establish and maintain a complete and adequate system of public education, and shall provide at least free public primary instruction, and citizenship training to adult citizens. All schools shall aim to develop moral character, personal discipline, civic conscience, and vocational efficiency, and to teach the duties of citizenship. Optional religious instruction shall be maintained in the public schools as now authorized by law. Universities established by the State shall enjoy academic freedom. They shall create scholarship in arts, science, and letters for specially gifted citizens."

The President of the Philippines cannot make any exception in favor of any one."[5]

The reasons for such state regulation of educational institutions are: 1) education is essentially a public affair;[6] 2) in order that schools may not become the possible agencies of subversive doctrine, inimical to the general welfare of the nation;[7] 3) in order to guarantee that the children attending private schools may be diligently prepared to fulfill their civic duties as citizens of the country;[8] 4) in order to protect the people from being exploited by educational institutions operated only for profit.[9]

ARTICLE II. DOCTRINE OF THE CHURCH ON EDUCATION

The Church teaches that education, being neither a private nor individual function, but essentially social and public, must be undertaken mutually by the three societies, the family, the Church and the State.[10]

The family—the primary end of marriage is not only the procreation of children, but likewise the education thereof.[11] Marriage has been instituted for the generation and formation of offspring; for this reason it has priority of nature and, therefore, of rights over civil society.[12] Since the family does not possess all the necessary means to provide for all its needs, and in particular for an adequate education of the offspring, the aid of the Church and the civil society is indispensable.

The Church—The duty of teaching is incumbent upon the Church for three reasons. 1) It is imposed by the mission entrusted to it by Jesus Christ to teach all nations. "All power

---

[5] Rodriquez, Eulogio B., *President Quezon His Biographical Sketch, Messages and Speeches* (Publishers Incorporated, Manila, Philippines, 1940), p. 146.

[6] Osias, "The Constitution and Education"—*Tribune* (Manila, June 6, 1935). Cf. Villarruz, *op. cit.*, p. 110.

[7] Aruego, *op. cit.*, vol. II, p. 615.

[8] Hayden, *The Philippines*, pp. 549, 550.

[9] *Ibid.*

[10] Pius XI, Encyclical, *"Divini illius Magistri"* (December 31, 1929)—*AAS*, XXII, 52.

[11] Canon 1013: "Matrimonii finis primarius est procreatio atque educatio prolis. . . ."

[12] Pius XI, Encyclical, *"Divini illius Magistri"*—*loc. cit.*, pp. 52-53.

is given to me in heaven and in earth. Going therefore teach ye all nations, baptizing them in the name of the Father, and of the Son, and of the Holy Ghost, teaching them to observe all things whatsoever I have commanded you, and behold I am with you all days, even to the consummation of the world."[13] 2) It derives from the Church's supernatural motherhood.[14] The Church becomes the mother of all those who, through the regenerating waters of baptism, are born into this supernatural family, and are nurtured and educated in the supernatural life with her doctrine. "He has not God for Father," says St. Augustine, "who refuses to have the Church as mother."[15]

In matters of faith and morals the right of the Church to teach is exclusive and completely independent of any earthly power. In faith and morals, God Himself has made the Church sharer in the divine magisterium and, by divine privilege, granted her immunity from error; hence, she is the mistress of men, supreme and absolutely sure, and she has inherent in herself an invincible right to freedom in teaching.[16] In other fields of learning the right of the Church is not exclusive. 3) It flows from the Church's juridical perfection. The Church has the right arising from its juridic nature to teach independently of any civil interference, even in matters, which do not have any connection with faith and morals. Hence, "the Church is independent of any sort of earthly power as well in the origin as in the exercise of her mission as educator, not merely in regard to her proper end and object, but also in regard to the means necessary and suitable to attain that end. Hence, with regard to every kind of human learning and instruction, which is the common patrimony of individuals and society, the Church has an independent right to make use of it, and above all to decide what may help or harm Christian education."[17]

---

[13] Matth.; XXVIII, 18-20.

[14] Pius XI, Encyclical, *"Divini illius Magistri"—loc. cit.*, p. 54.

[15] De symbolo sermo ad catechumenos. Cf. Migne, *Patres Latini,* XL, c. XIII, n. 13.

[16] Leo XIII, Encyclical, *"Libertas Praestantissimum"* (June 20, 1888)—*ASS,* XX, 607.

[17] Pius XI, Encyclical, *"Divini illius Magistri"* (December 31, 1929)—*ASS,* XXII, 54.

Thus, the right of the Church of founding and maintaining educational institutions in all branches of learning is emphatically guaranteed by the sacred canons.[18] It is also the inalienable right of the Church to exercise its maternal supervision over the entire education of children attending both public and private institutions not only in matters of religion, but also in other branches of learning which have relation with faith and morals.[19]

This seemingly arrogant claim of the Church by no means signifies undue interference in State affairs, or a challenge to State regulations on matters of education, but rather its solicitude in protecting the sound education of its members from false doctrine. As a matter of fact "the Church in her maternal prudence is not unwilling that her schools and institutions for the education of the laity be in keeping with the legitimate dispositions of civil authority; she is in many ways ready to cooperate with this authority and to make provision for mutual understanding, should difficulties arise."[20] This good will of the Church is frequently manifested in Concordats.[21] In these treaties with nations the Church permits her schools to be subject to the State regulations, as for example, to the general program of studies and system of lectures planned by the government.

The State—It is the duty of the State to protect and foster education. Since the function of the government in this matter, is essentially subsidiary and, by no means, monopolizing and absorbing, it is its duty to protect by its laws the rights of the family and the Church in the exercise of their mission as educators to whom the task of teaching has been particularly entrusted;

---

[18] Canon 1375: "Ecclesiae est ius scholas cuiusvis disciplinae non solum elementarias, sed etiam medias et superiores condendi."

[19] Canon 1381, § 1: "Religiosa iuventutis institutio in scholis quibusvis auctoritati et inspectioni Ecclesiae subiicitur." § 2. Ordinariis locorum ius et officium est vigilandi ne in quibusvis scholis sui territorii quidquam contra fidem vel bonos mores tradatur aut fiat." Cf. 1382.

[20] Pius XI, Encyclical, *"Divini illius Magistri"* (December 31, 1929)—*AAS,* XXII (1930), 56.

[21] Concordat with Italy (February 11, 1929), art. 35—*AAS,* XXI (1929), 291; Concordat with Romania (May 10, 1927), art. 19—*AAS,* XXI (1929), 449; Concordat with Austria (June 5, 1933), art. 4—*AAS,* XXVI (1934), 257.

and to protect the rights of the child itself whenever the parents are unable either physically or morally to fulfill their obligation in this respect.[22]

Inasmuch as education is one of the most effective means for the attainment of the general prosperity of the nation, its promotion becomes a strict obligation on the part of the government. "It should begin by encouraging and assisting, of its own accord, the initiative and activity of the Church and the family, whose successes in this field have been clearly demonstrated by history and experience. It should, moreover, supplement their work whenever this falls short of what is necessary, even by means put at its disposal for the needs of all, and it is only right that it use these means to the advantage of those who have contributed them."[23] Finally, the State can enforce special measures for the training of citizens in their civic and political duties, and for the development of their intellectual and moral character. To this effect, it can reserve to itself the direction of all the institutions which aim to prepare the youth for civic duties, v.g., for military service, provided that in such an enterprise the rights of the Church and the family are respected.[24]

The Constitution of the Philippines in its educational provision is in accordance with the teachings of the Church, in as much as it recognizes the inalienable rights of the family regarding the education of the children and guarantees to the parents the support of the government. It failed, however, to render assistance and support to the Church in its activities in the field of education. The Constitution expressly prohibits the employment of public funds for the benefit of any institution which promotes religion.[25]

In the opinion of the writer the support of the Philippine government given to Catholic schools would be just both to the Church and to the citizens, apart from the fact that it has *"a*

---

[22] Pius XI, Encyclical, *"Divini illius Magistri," ibid.*, 63.

[23] Pius XI, Encyclical, *"Divini illius Magistri," ibid.*, 63.

[24] Pius XI, Encyclical, *"Divini illius Magistri," ibid.*, 64.

[25] The Constitution of the Philippines (1935), art. VI, sec. 13 (2). Cf. Aruego, *Know Your Constitution* (University Publishing Co., Inc., Manila, Philippines, 1940), pp. 100, 101.

priori" an obligation to render it. If all the faithful are bound by a strict obligation to support the Catholic schools,[26] the stricter must be the duty of the State, since it is greatly benefited by the Christian culture imparted by the Church through its schools.[27]

Since the discovery of the Islands, the Church, side by side with the government, has played an important role in the cultural development of the Filipino people; as a matter of fact the Catholic schools are held by the Filipinos in very high esteem not only because they possess good standards, but especially because the majority of the leaders in the government, scholars and outstanding professional men are alumni of Catholic institutions.[28]

The support of the government given to private schools would be only fair dealing with its citizens. Catholics, as other citizens, give their proportionate contribution for the support of the national school system which, being neutral, they cannot in conscience use without some special justifying cause. Catholics are forbidden to send their children to neutral schools.[29] Catholics face, if they send their children to private schools, a double financial burden by supporting two school systems. From this it follows that poor parents who cannot afford the luxury of a private school are forced to send their children to public ones.[30]

Most of the outstanding Filipino families and statesmen, they who bitterly oppose any sort of Church influence in public instruction, send their own children nevertheless to Catholic colleges and universities.

Would government support of any kind given to Catholic and other private educational institutions violate the principles of democracy? The answer would be the following. In countries which are claimed as champions of democracy, v.g., in the United

---

[26] Canon 1379, § 3: "Fideles ne omittant adiutricem operam pro viribus conferre in catholicas scholas condendas et sustentendas."

[27] Leo XIII, Encyclical, "*Sapientiae Christianae*" (January 10, 1890)—*ASS,* XXII (1889-1890), 389. Ottaviani, *Institutiones Iuris Publici Ecclesiastici,* II, 245.

[28] Hayden, *The Philippines,* p. 554.

[29] Canon 1374: "Pueri catholici scholas acatholicas, nuetras, mixtas, quae nempe etiam acatholicas patent, ne frequentent."

[30] Hayden, *op. cit.,* p. 566.

States of America, sectarian schools receive some help from the public funds. The Constitution of New York of 1938, art. II, sec. 4 provides bus transportation for children attending both church and government schools.[31] The Louisiana Supreme Court upheld as constitutional the statute providing text books for pupils of both private and public schools.[32]

The tax power of the nation is exacted for public purposes and interests. And Catholic schools are established precisely for the common welfare of the people as a whole. They are not operated for egoistic purposes. "If Catholics build parochial schools while supporting public schools, it is not because they are opposed to what the latter teach, for both teach the same; it is only because of what is left out; it is because Christ, who blessed the little children, who taught them and who still teaches them if they come to Him, is left out from the whole scheme of things."[33]

It is only right and fair, therefore, that the State, being provided by the citizens with more means than any other society, should give its support to private schools, for in doing this it would use the means put at its disposal for the advantage of those who have contributed them.[34]

ARTICLE III. RELIGIOUS INSTRUCTION IN PUBLIC SCHOOLS

When the Constitutional Convention came to the drafting of a provision concerning religious instruction in the public schools, the members of the Convention were divided into three groups, each holding a different position on this particular subject. Some advocated the complete prohibition of religious instruction; others

---

[31] Dec. 26, 1938, "League for Separation of Church and State"—New York Times.

[32] Cochran v. Louisiana State Board of Education, 168 La. 1030, 123. So. 664 (1929) Further examples can be found in "*The Jurist*"—see index for Oct. 1943 under "subsidy," "text books" and "transportation."

[33] Spellman, *The Road to Victory* (New York, Charles Scribner's Sons, 1942), p. 32.

[34] Cf. Gabel, *Public Funds for Church and Private Schools* (Toledo, 1937). This is a thorough study on the question of State support for Catholic schools.

maintained that it should be placed within the regular curriculum, and that it should be taken only by pupils whose parents or guardians desire so; and others were of the opinion that the provision of optional religious instruction as provided by the present law should be maintained.[85]

At the final vote, the members of the Convention adopted the opinion of those who held the continuance of the optional religious instruction as authorized by the present law. According to Delegates Esliza and Castro the teaching of religion in the public schools as a part of the curriculum would violate the principle of separation of Church and State; religion should be taught at home, in the Church or in other places; the teachers of religion, taking advantage of their position as professors in religion, might inculcate into the minds of the pupils doctrine pernicious both to the State and religion itself.[86]

The Catholic Church has never been completely contented with the present legislation, because of the insufficiency and inconvenience of the time granted, and of the unsatisfactory enforcement of the law itself.[87] The people themselves want their children to be given more religious instruction than is provided by the present law. Furthermore, they are not satisfied with the civil system of character training of the public schools.[88] This moral and character building aimed at by the public instruction

---

[85] Hayden, *op. cit.*, p. 565: Administrative Code of 1917, sec. 929. "It should be lawful, however, for the priest or minister of any church established in the town where a public school is situated, either in person or by a designated teacher of religion, to teach religion for one-half hour three times a week, in the school building, to those public-school pupils whose parents or guardians desire it and express their desire therefor in writing filed with the principal teacher of the school, to be forwarded to the division superintendent, who shall fix the hours and rooms for such teaching. But no public-school teachers shall either conduct religious exercises or teach religion or act as a designated religious teacher in the school building under the foregoing authority, and no pupils shall be required by any public-school teacher to attend and receive the religious instruction herein permitted."

[86] Aruego, *The Framing of the Philippine Constitution,* II, 628.

[87] Hayden, *op. cit.*, p. 567.

[88] *Ibid.*, p. 566.

is given independently of religion; the teachers are strictly forbidden to use religious influence.[39]

Many Filipino families send their children to Catholic schools just because of the religious instruction they receive therein. "In all probability the proportion would be still higher among the poorer people who cannot afford the luxury of a private school."[40]

In view of these facts it was not any surprise at all that the National Assembly passed a bill on May 12, 1938, providing religious instruction within the regular curriculum in all public schools.[41]

President Quezon, although he himself is very much in favor of religious instruction for children, vetoed the bill on the ground that it was unconstitutional.[42] "It may not be amiss," he said in his veto message, "to reiterate that I am one of those who believe that religious instruction is not only good, but necessary

---

[39] Administrative Code, sec. 927: "No teacher or other person engaged in any public school, whether maintained from Insular, provincial or municipal funds, shall teach or criticize the doctrines of any church, religious sect, or denomination, or shall attempt to influence the pupils for or against any church or religious sect."

[40] Hayden, *op. cit.*, p. 566.

[41] Bill 3307. Cf. Hayden, *op. cit.*, pp. 565-566; Bill 3307, sec. 1: "There shall be included in the curriculum of all of the public schools of the Philippines from the lowest grade to the highest year of the High or vocational school, inclusive under the direct supervision of the school authorities, a course in character building and good manners and right conduct. This course shall be a subject, scheduled during regular school hours, and instruction therein shall be given for one-half hour three times a week throughout the academic year. . . ."

Sec. 2: "Where any religious organization or organizations are in a position to offer religious instruction with their own instructors, and at no cost to the government, parents or guardians of minor children under parental authority in public schools shall, upon written request filed with the principal teacher of the school, have the right to have their children excused from the instruction in character building and good manners and right conduct as provided in section one hereof, and on the condition that said children attend the religious instruction offered by the religious organization or organizations chosen by the parents, all in accordance with the law."

[42] In a message of the President to the National Assembly (June 4, 1938). Cf. Rodriquez, *President Quezon his Biographical Sketch—Messages and Speeches*, p. 168.

for children of school age. I consider religion as a great power for good. It is stabilizing in its influence. It is good for the individual and good for the body politic."[43]

Under the optional religious instruction the Church is permitted to teach religion in all the public schools but without any financial help from the government and outside the regular curriculum. Although the Church does not have at her disposal the means which the government possesses in the fulfillment of its mission in this respect, nevertheless, in 1938 religious instruction was being given in 817 public schools to 187,089 pupils.[44]

ARTICLE IV. MARRIAGE

Another question of joint jurisdiction is marriage. Matrimony as a sacrament is exclusively governed by the canonical legislation and in its mere civil effects by the State.[45]

The Philippine Constitution does not make any provision for marriage. It is provided, by the "Marriage Law" of December 4, 1929, no. 3613. Civil marriage is at the option of the contracting parties; they are free to solemnize their wedding before the Church or before the civil magistrate.

Divorce is also permitted by the State and it is regulated by the "Act No. 2710," a law enacted by the Philippine Legislature.[46]

---

[43] Rodriquez, *op. cit.*, p. 182.

[44] Hayden, *op. cit.*, p. 567.

[45] Canon 1016: "Baptizatorum matrimonium regitur iure non solum divino, sed etiam canonico, salva competentia civilis potestatis circa mere civiles eiusdem matrimonii effectus."

[46] Fisher, F. C., *The Civil Code of Spain with Philippine Notes and References.* Translation from Spanish, 4. ed.; Manila, P. I. and Rochester, N. Y., 1930.

CHAPTER XIV

Conclusions

1) The Philippine Constitution of 1935 in its aim and means to attain that end is in conformity with the principles of the Christian Constitution of States.

2) The separation of Church and State established by the Constitution of the Philippine Commonwealth does not perfectly conform to the principles of Christian philosophy which consider the separation of the two powers permissible only in special circumstances. Since it does not recognize the Church as a perfect society, all the privileges and rights now enjoyed by the Catholic Church in the Philippines are considered as liberal concessions on the part of the State.

3) In some matters of common jurisdiction the Philippine legislation has passed beyond the limits of its respective field of action, v.g., by civil divorce it dissolves the very sacramental bond of marriage, permitting the parties to marry again.

4) In order that the religious instruction within the regular curriculum would not be unconstitutional under the present legislation, and in view of the general will of the people that their children be instructed in religion to a greater extent than is permitted by the present law, it would be a wise policy to amend the constitutional provision on this subject, as it has been done in regard to the presidential term of office.

5) The Philippine Constitution enforced by men imbued with Christian principles would be as beneficial to the welfare of the Church as it would be pernicious to her if enforced by atheistic statesmen.

6) The expression, "union of Church and State," seems popularly to mean more today than it really signifies, suggesting the idea of the fusion of the two powers.

BIBLIOGRAPHY

Sources

Acta Apostolicae Sedis, Commentarium Officiale, Romae, Typis Polyglottis, 1909-

Acta Leonis XIII (1878-1903), (23 vols., Romae, 1881-1905).

Acta Sanctae Sedis, 41 vols., Romae, 1865-1908.

Codex Iuris Canonici Pii X Pontificis Maximi iussu digestus Benedicti Papae XV auctoritate promulgatus, Typis Polyglottis Vaticanis, 1917.

Codicis Iuris Canonici Fontes cura Em̃. Petri Card. Gasparri editi, 9 vols., Romae [postea Civitate Vaticana]: Typis Polyglottis Vaticanis, 1923-1939. (Vols. VII-IX ed. cura et studio Em̃i. Justiniani Card. Serédi.)

Constitution of the Philippine Commonwealth (1935).

Denzinger, H., Enchiridion Symbolorum Definitionum et Declarationum de Rebus Fidei et Morum, quod a Clemente Bannwart denuo compositum iteratis curis edidit Johannes Bapt. Umberg, S.J., 10-20 ed., Friburgi Brisgoviae, 1932: Herder & Co. Typographi Editoris Pontificii.

Reference Works

Aegidius Romanus, *De Potestate Ecclesiastica,* edited by Richard S. Weimar, Herman Boehlaus, 1929.

Aquinas, Thomas, *Summa Theologica,* 6 vols., Taurini, Italia: Marietti, 1928.

———, *Summa Theologica,* translation by the Fathers of the English Dominican Province (Benziger Brothers, New York, 1913-1937).

Aristotle, *Politics,* English translation by Jowett, Oxford, Clarendon Press, 1905.

Aruego, José M., *The Framing of the Philippine Constitution,* 2 vols.: University Publishing Co., Inc., Manila, Philippines, 1936.

———, *Know Your Constitution:* University Publishing Co., Inc., Manila, Philippines, 1940.

Atheistic Communism, Washington, National Catholic Welfare Conference, 1937.

Baradi, Mauro, *The Commonwealth of the Philippines to Date,* Washington, D. C., 1939.

Bellarminus, Robertus, *De Laicis, or the Treatise on Civil Government.* Translated by Murphy, K. E., New York, Fordham University Press, 1928.

———, *Opera Omnia,* editio nova juxta Venetam anni 1721, 8 vols., Neapoli: C. Pedone Lauriel Editor.

Billot, L., *Tractatus de Ecclesia Christi*, 2 vols., Prati, 1910: ex officina Libraria Giachetti, Filii et Soc.

———, *De Habitudine Ecclesiae ad Civilem Societatem*, Prati, 1910.

Boffa, Conrad Humbert, *Canonical Provisions for Catholic Schools*, The Catholic University of America Canon Law Studies, No. 117, Washington, D. C.: The Catholic University Press, 1939.

Bossuet, J., *Controverse, Œuvres Complètes*, 52 vols., a Paris: Chez Gauthier Frères et C, Librairies, 1878.

Brosnahan, *Prolegomena to Ethics with a Digest of Ethics*, edited by Le Buffe, New York, 1941.

Burlamaqui, *The Principles of Natural and Political Law*, translated into English by Nugent, 5 ed., Cambridge: The University Press, 1776.

Bustos, Felixberto G. and Fajardo, Abelardo J., *The New Philippines* (Carmelo & Bauermann, Inc.: Publishers, Manila, Philippines, 1934).

Cahill, E., *The Framework of a Christian State*, Dublin: M. H. Gill and Son, Ltd., 1932.

Cappello, Felix M., *Summa Iuris Publici Ecclesiastici*, 4. ed., Romae: Apud Aedes Universitatis Gregorianae, 1932.

———, *Summa Iuris Canonici*, 3 vols.; vol. I, 2. ed., 1932; vol. II, 2. ed., 1934; vol. III, 1936, Romae: Apud Aedes Universitatis Gregorianae.

Catholic Encyclopedia, The, 16 vols., New York, 1907-1914.

Cathrein, Victor, *Moralphilosophie*, 2. ed., 2 vols., Freiburg im Breisgau, 1893.

———, *Philosophia Moralis in Usum Scholarum*, 6. ed., Freiburg Brisgoviae, Herder: Typographi Editoris Pontificii, 1907.

Cavagnis, Felix, *Institutiones Iuris Publici Ecclesiastici*, 2. ed., Romae: Typis Societatis Catholicae Instructivae, 1888.

Colleción de Encíclicas y Otras Cartas de los Papas Gregorio XVI, Leo XIII, Pio X, Benedicto XV y Pio XI, con otros documentos episcopales y maxima autoridad sobre doctrina política, social, educación, familia y acción católica, compilados, anotados y ordenados sus conceptos en un índice alfabetico, Madrid: Imp. "Saes hermanos," 1935.

Coronata, Mathaeus, Conte a, *Institutiones Iuris Canonici*, 5 vols.; vols. I-II, 2. ed., 1939; vols., III-IV, 1933-1936, Taurini: Marietti.

Cronin, Michael, *The Science of Ethics*, vol. I, 1920; vol. II, 1917, New York, Benziger.

Del Giudice, Vincenzo, *Corso di Diritto Ecclesiastico*, 1929-1930, Milano: Stab. Tipo-Litografico G. Tenconi.

Discorsi e Radiomessagi di Sua Santitá Pio XII, 2 vols., Milano, Societá editrice "Vita e Pensiero," 1941.

Doyle, J., *Education in Recent Constitutions and Concordats*, Washington: The Catholic University of America, 1933.

Dunning, W. A., *A History of Political Theories from Rousseau to Spencer*, N. Y., Macmillan, 1920.

Farges et Barbedette, *Philosophia Scholastica,* 55. ed., 2 vols., Pariis: Apud Berche et Pagis, Editores, 1932.

Fisher, F. C., *The Civil Code of Spain with Philippine Notes and References.* Translation from Spanish, 4. ed.: Manila, P. I., and Rochester, N. Y., 1930.

Foundations for Peace. Letters of Pope Pius XII and President Roosevelt, London, Catholic Truth Society, 1940.

Gillis, James M., *The Church and Modern Thought*: Washington, D. C., 1935.

Goodnow, F. J., *Social Reform and the Constitution*: New York, The Macmillan Company, 1911.

Great Encyclical Letters of Pope Leo XIII, The, with preface by Rev. John J. Wynne, S.J.: New York, Benziger Brothers, 1903.

Guenechea, Joseph N., *Principia Iuris Politici,* 2 vols., Romae: Apud Aedes Universitatis Gregorianae, 1939.

Haas, Francis J., *Man and Society,* New York: D. Appleton-Century Company, 1930.

Hayden, J., *The Philippines,* New York: Macmillan Company, 1942.

Hobbes, T., *Elementaria Philosophia de Cive,* Amstelodami, 1696.

Jesuitas, Algunos Padres, *El Archipiélago Filipino,* Collección de datos, geográficos, estadísticos, cronológicos y científicos, relativos al mismo, entresacados de anteriores obras u obtenidos con la propria observación y estudio, 2 vols.: Washington, D. C., 1900.

Kalaw, Maximo M., *The Development of Philippine Politics,* Manila, P. I., 1900.

Koenig, Joseph C., *Principles for Peace, Selections from Papal Documents, Leo XIII to Pius XII*: National Catholic Welfare Conference, Washington, D. C., 1943.

Kremer, Michael, *Church Support in the United States,* The Catholic University of America Canon Law Studies, No. 61, Washington, D. C.: The Catholic University of America, 1930.

Le Buffe and Hayes, *Jurisprudence,* New York, 1938.

Liberatore, Mathieu, *Le Droit Public de l'Eglise,* traduit de l'Italien, avec l'autorisation speciale de l'Auteur, par M. Aug. Onclair, Prêtre, Paris: Retaux-Bray, Libraire-Editeur, 1888.

Lo Grasso, Giovanni B., *Ecclesia et Status, De mutuis officiis et iuribus fontes selecti,* Romae: Apud Aedes Universitatis Gregorianae, 1939.

Mabini, Apolinario, *La Revolución Filipina,* 2 vols., Manila, P. I.: Bureau of Printing, 1931.

Makée, P. Ch., *Institutiones Iuris Ecclesiastici,* 2 vols., Parisiis: Apud A. Roger et F. Chernoviz, 1897.

Malcolm and Laurel, *The Constitutional Law of the Philippines,* 3. ed.; The Lawyer Co-operative Publishing Company, Manila, P. I., Rochester, N. Y., 1936.

Messages of President [*Quezon*], 5 vols., Manila: Bureau of Printing, 1938.

Mexican Persecution, The, The Encyclical *"Acerba Animi,"* London, Catholic Truth Society, 1932.

Meyer, Theodorus, *Institutiones Iuris Naturalis,* St. Louis: Herder Company, 1906.

Migne, Jacques Paul, *Patrologiae Cursus Completus, Series Latina,* 221 vols., Pariisis, 1844-1864.

Morales, V., *Ensayo de una Síntesis de los Trabajos Realizados por las Corporaciones Religiosas Españoles de Filipinas,* 2 vols.: Manila, P. I., 1901.

Moulart, F. I., *L'Eglise et L'Etat,* 4. ed., Paris, 1895.

Ottaviani, Alaphridus, *Institutiones Iuris Publici Ecclesiastici,* 2. ed., 2 vols.: Typis Polyglottis Vaticanis, 1935-1936.

Pelagius, Alvarus, *De Planctu Ecclesiae,* 2 vols., in 1: Venetiis, F. Sansvini et Sociorum, 1560.

Pope's Five Peace-Points, The, Allocution to the College of Cardinals by His Holiness, Pope Pius XII, December 24, 1939: London, Catholic Truth Society, 1940.

Rankin, Charles, *The Pope Speaks,* The words of Pius XII, Rattway, N. Y., Quinn & Boden Company, Inc., 1940.

Rodriquez, Eulogio B., *President Quezon his Biographical Sketch—Messages and Speeches*: Publishers Incorporated Manila-P. I., 1940.

Rousseau, J. J., *Du Contrat Social,* Paris, 1793.

Ryan, John A., and Boland, Francis J., *Catholic Principles of Politics* (Revised Edition of *The State and the Church*), New York: The Macmillan Company, 1941.

Spellman, Francis J., *The Road to Victory,* New York, Charles Scribner's Sons, 1942.

Suarez, F., *Opera Omnia,* ed. nova, a Carolo Berton, 26 vols., Pariis: Apud Ludovicum Vives, Bibliopolam Editorem, 1859.

Taparelli, *Droit Naturel* (translated from Italian into French by M. l'abbè C. A. Ozanam), Paris, 1863.

Tarquini, Camillus, *Iuris Ecclesiastici Publici Institutiones,* 4. ed., Romae: Typographia Polyglotta, 1852.

Vermeersch, A., *Tolerance,* translated by Humphrey, Page W.: Benziger Brothers, N. Y., 1913.

Vermeersch-Cruesen, *Epitome Iuris Canonici,* 3 vols., vol. I, 6. ed., 1937; vol. II, 5. ed., 1934; vol. III, 5. ed., 1936: Mechliniae et Romae, Dessain.

Villarruz, N. V., *Commentaries and Opinions on the Constitution of the Philippines*: Manila, P. I., 1935.

Woywod, Stanislaus, *A Practical Commentary on the Code of Canon Law,* 5. ed., 2 vols.: New York, Jos. F. Wagner, 1939.

Zollmann, C., *American Church Law,* St. Paul: West Publishing Co., 1933.

Zapelena, Timotheus, *De Ecclesia Christi, Pars Apologetica,* Romae: Apud Aedes Universitatis Gregorianae, 1940.

Periodicals

Catholic Mind, The, New York, 1903-
Civiltá Cattolica, La, Roma, 1850-
Irish Ecclesiastical Record, The, Dublin, 1864-
Jurist, The, The Catholic University of America, 1941-
Razón y Fe, Madrid, 1901-
Religión y Cultura, Real Monasterio de El Escorial y Madrid, Columela, 1928-
Tablet, The, London, 1840-
Theological Studies, The American Press, New York, N. Y., 1943-
Thought, Fordham University, 1926-
Unitas, The organ of the Faculty of the University of Sto. Tomas, Manila, P. I.

Newspapers

Philippine Herald, The, Manila, P. I.
Sunday Herald, Manila, P. I.
Sunday Tribune, Manila, P. I.
New York Times, New York, N. Y.

BIOGRAPHICAL NOTE

Alexander Ayson Olalia was born at Bacolar, Pampanga, Philippine Islands, February 26, 1913. His elementary and high school education was received in his own Province. In 1930 he entered the Diocesan Seminary of St. Charles, Manila, P. I. After finishing philosophy in 1936, he was sent to the Gregorian University, Rome, Italy, where he completed his theological course receiving the S.T.L. degree. After ordination to the priesthood in 1940, he entered the School of Canon Law at the same University where he received the Licentiate in Canon Law in June, 1942. In the same year he came to the United States through an exchange of citizens between the belligerents. He spent one year in the missions of Georgia. In 1943 he entered the School of Canon Law at the Catholic University of America.

CANON LAW STUDIES*

1. FRERIKS, REV. CELESTINE A., C.PP.S., J.C.D., Religious Congregations in Their External Relations, 121 pp., 1916.
2. GALLIHER, REV. DANIEL M., O.P., J.C.D., Canonical Elections, 117 pp., 1917.
3. BORKOWSKI, REV. AURELIUS L., O.F.M., J.C.D., De Confraternitatibus Ecclesiasticis, 136 pp., 1918.
4. CASTILLO, REV. CAYO, J.C.D., Disertacion Historico-Canonica sobre la Potestad del Cabildo en Sede Vacante o Impedida del Vicario Capitular, 99 pp., 1919 (1918).
5. KUBELBECK, REV. WILLIAM J., S.T.B., J.C.D., The Sacred Penitentiaria and Its Relation to Faculties of Ordinaries and Priests, 129 pp., 1918.
6. PETROVITS, REV. JOSEPH J. C., S.T.D., J.C.D., The New Church Law on Matrimony, X-461 pp., 1919.
7. HICKEY, REV. JOHN J., S.T.B., J.C.D., Irregularities and Simple Impediments in the New Code of Canon Law, 100 pp., 1920.
8. KLEKOTKA, REV. PETER J., S.T.B., J.C.D., Diocesan Consultors, 179 pp., 1920.
9. WANENMACHER, REV. FRANCIS, J.C.D., The Evidence in Ecclesiastical Procedure Affecting the Marriage Bond, 1920 (Printed 1935).
10. GOLDEN, REV. HENRY FRANCIS, J.C.D., Parochial Benefices in the New Code, IV-119 pp., 1921 (Printed 1925).
11. KOUDELKA, REV. CHARLES J., J.C.D., Pastors, Their Rights and Duties According to the New Code of Canon Law, 211 pp., 1921.
12. MELO, REV. ANTONIUS, O.F.M., J.C.D., De Exemptione Regularium, X-188 pp., 1921.
13. SCHAAF, REV. VALENTINE THEODORE, O.F.M., S.T.B., J.C.D., The Cloister, X-180 pp., 1921.
14. BURKE, REV. THOMAS JOSEPH, S.T.D., J.C.D., Competence in Ecclesiastical Tribunals, IV-117 pp., 1922.
15. LEECH, REV. GEORGE LEO, J.C.D., A Comparative Study of the Constitution "Apostolicae Sedis" and the "Codex Juris Canonici," 179 pp., 1922.
16. MOTRY, REV. HUBERT LOUIS, S.T.D., J.C.D., Diocesan Faculties According to the Code of Canon Law, II-167 pp., 1922.
17. MURPHY, REV. GEORGE LAWRENCE, J.C.D., Delinquencies and Penalties in the Administration and the Reception of the Sacraments, IV-121 pp., 1923.

* Below n. 100 only the following numbers are still available: Nn. 3, 4, 9, 25, 34, 57 and 75. Beginning with n. 100 only the following are unavailable: Nn. 100-111 inclusive, and n. 118.

18. O'Reilly, Rev. John Anthony, S.T.B., J.C.D., Ecclesiastical Sepulture in the New Code of Canon Law, 11-129 pp., 1923.
19. Michalicka, Rev. Wenceslas Cyril, O.S.B., J.C.D., Judicial Procedure in Dismissal of Clerical Exempt Religious, 107 pp., 1923.
20. Dargin, Rev. Edward Vincent, S.T.B., J.C.D., Reserved Cases According to the Code of Canon Law, IV-103 pp., 1924.
21. Godfrey, Rev. John A., S.T.B., J.C.D., The Right of Patronage According to the Code of Canon Law, 153 pp., 1924.
22. Hagedorn, Rev. Francis Edward, J.C.D., General Legislation on Indulgences, II-154 pp., 1924.
23. King, Rev. James Ignatius, J.C.D., The Administration of the Sacraments to Dying Non-Catholics, V-141 pp., 1924.
24. Winslow, Rev. Francis Joseph, O.F.M., J.C.D., Vicars and Prefects Apostolic, IV-149 pp., 1924.
25. Correa, Rev. Jose Servelion, S.T.L., J.C.D., La Potestad Legislativa de la Iglesia Catolica, IV-127 pp., 1925.
26. Dugan, Rev. Henry Francis, A.M., J.C.D., The Judiciary Department of the Diocesan Curia, 87 pp., 1925.
27. Keller, Rev. Charles Frederick, S.T.B., J.C.D., Mass Stipends, 167 pp., 1925.
28. Paschang, Rev. John Linus, J.C.D., The Sacramentals According to the Code of Canon Law, 129 pp., 1925.
29. Piontek, Rev. Cyrillus, O.F.M., S.T.B., J.C.D., De Indulto Exclaustrationis necnon Saecularizationis, XIII-289 pp., 1925.
30. Kearney, Rev. Richard Joseph, S.T.B., J.C.D., Sponsors at Baptism According to the Code of Canon Law, IV-127 pp., 1925.
31. Bartlett, Rev. Chester Joseph, A.M., LL.B., J.C.D., The Tenure of Parochial Property in the United States of America, V-108 pp., 1926.
32. Kilker, Rev. Adrian Jerome, J.C.D., Extreme Unction, V-425 pp., 1926.
33. McCormick, Rev. Robert Emmett, J.C.D., Confessors of Religious, VIII-266 pp., 1926.
34. Miller, Rev. Newton Thomas, J.C.D., Founded Masses According to the Code of Canon Law, VII-93 pp., 1926.
35. Roelker, Rev. Edward G., S.T.D., J.C.D., Principles of Privilege According to the Code of Canon Law, XI-166 pp., 1926.
36. Bakalarczyk, Rev. Richardus, M.I.C., J.U.D., De Novitiatu, VIII-208 pp., 1927.
37. Pizzuti, Rev. Lawrence, O.F.M., J.U.L., De Parochis Religiosis, 1927. (Not Printed.)
38. Bliley, Rev. Nicholas Martin, O.S.B., J.C.D., Altars According to the Code of Canon Law, XIX-132 pp., 1927.
39. Brown, Mr. Brendan Francis, A.B., LL.M., J.U.D., The Canonical Juristic Personality with Special Reference to its Status in the United States of America, V-212 pp., 1927.

40. Cavanaugh, Rev. William Thomas, C.P., J.U.D., The Reservation of the Blessed Sacrament, VIII-101 pp., 1927.
41. Doheny, Rev. William J., C.S.C., A.B., J.U.D., Church Property: Modes of Acquisition, X-118 pp., 1927.
42. Feldhaus, Rev. Aloysius H., C.PP.S., J.C.D., Oratories, IX-141 pp., 1927.
43. Kelly, Rev. James Patrick, A.B., J.C.D., The Jurisdiction of the Simple Confessor, X-208 pp., 1927.
44. Neuberger, Rev. Nicholas J., J.C.D., Canon 6 or the Relation of the Codex Juris Canonici to the Preceding Legislation, V-95 pp., 1927.
45. O'Keefe, Rev. Gerald Michael, J.C.D., Matrimonial Dispensations, Powers of Bishops, Priests, and Confessors, VIII-232 pp., 1927.
46. Quigley, Rev. Joseph A. M., A.B., J.C.D., Condemned Societies, 139 pp., 1927.
47. Zaplotnik, Rev. Johannes Leo, J.C.D., De Vicariis Foraneis, X-142 pp., 1927.
48. Duskie, Rev. John Aloysius, A.B., J.C.D., The Canonical Status of the Orientals in the United States, VIII-196 pp., 1928.
49. Hyland, Rev. Francis Edward, J.C.D., Excommunication, Its Nature, Historical Development and Effects, VIII-181 pp., 1928.
50. Reinmann, Rev. Gerald Joseph, O.M.C., J.C.D., The Third Order Secular of Saint Francis, 201 pp., 1928.
51. Schenk, Rev. Francis J., J.C.D., The Matrimonial Impediments of Mixed Religion and Disparity of Cult, XVI-318 pp., 1929.
52. Coady, Rev. John Joseph, S.T.D., J.U.D., A.M., The Appointment of Pastors, VIII-150 pp., 1929.
53. Kay, Rev. Thomas Henry, J.C.D., Competence in Matrimonial Procedure, VIII-164 pp., 1929.
54. Turner, Rev. Sidney Joseph, C.P., J.U.D., The Vow of Poverty, XLIX-217 pp., 1929.
55. Kearney, Rev. Raymond A., A.B., S.T.D., J.C.D., The Principles of Delegation, VII-149 pp., 1929.
56. Conran, Rev. Edward James, A.B., J.C.D., The Interdict, V-163 pp., 1930.
57. O'Neill, Rev. William H., J.C.D., Papal Rescripts of Favor, VII-218 pp., 1930.
58. Bastnagel, Rev. Clement Vincent, J.U.D., The Appointment of Parochial Adjutants and Assistants, XV-257 pp., 1930.
59. Ferry, Rev. William A., A.B., J.C.D., Stole Fees, V-136 pp., 1930.
60. Costello, Rev. John Michael, A.B., J.C.D., Domicile and Quasi-Domicile, VII-201 pp., 1930.
61. Kremer, Rev. Michael Nicholas, A.B., S.T.B., J.C.D., Church Support in the United States, VI-136 pp., 1930.
62. Angulo, Rev. Luis, C.M., J.C.D., Legislation de la Iglesia sobre la intencion en la application de la Santa Misa, VII-104 pp., 1931.

63. FREY, REV. WOLFGANG NORBERT, O.S.B., A.B., J.C.D., The Act of Religious Profession, VIII-174 pp., 1931.
64. ROBERTS, REV. JAMES BRENDAN, A.B., J.C.D., The Banns of Marriage, XIV-140 pp., 1931.
65. RYDER, REV. RAYMOND ALOYSIUS, A.B., J.C.D., Simony, IX-151 pp., 1931.
66. CAMPAGNA, REV. ANGELO, PH.D., J.U.D., Il Vicario Generale del Vescovo, VII-205 pp., 1931.
67. COX, REV. JOSEPH GODFREY, A.B., J.C.D., The Administration of Seminaries, VI-124 pp., 1931.
68. GREGORY, REV. DONALD J., J.U.D., The Pauline Privilege, XV-165 pp., 1931.
69. DONOHUE, REV. JOHN F., J.C.D., The Impediment of Crime, VII-110 pp., 1931.
70. DOOLEY, REV. EUGENE A., O.M.I., J.C.D., Church Law on Sacred Relics, IX-143 pp., 1931.
71. ORTH, REV. CLEMENT RAYMOND, O.M.C., J.C.D., The Approbation of Religious Institutes, 171 pp., 1931.
72. PERNICONE, REV. JOSEPH M., A.B., J.C.D., The Ecclesiastical Prohibition of Books, XII-267 pp., 1932.
73. CLINTON, REV. CONNELL, A.B., J.C.D., The Paschal Precept, IX-108 pp., 1932.
74. DONNELLY, REV. FRANCIS B,. A.M., S.T.L., J.C.D., The Diocesan Synod, VIII-125 pp., 1932.
75. TORRENTE, REV. CAMILO, C.M.F., J.C.D., Las Procesiones Sagradas, V-145 pp., 1932.
76. MURPHY, REV. EDWIN J., C.PP.S., J.C.D., Suspension Ex Informata Conscientia, XI-122 pp., 1932.
77. MACKENZIE, REV. ERIC F., A.M., S.T.L., J.C.D., The Delict of Heresy in its Commission, Penalization, Absolution, VII-124 pp., 1932.
78. LYONS, REV. AVITUS E., S.T.B., J.C.D., The Collegiate Tribunal of First Instance, XI-147 pp., 1932.
79. CONNOLLY, REV. THOMAS A., J.C.D., Appeals, XI-195 pp., 1932.
80. SANGMEISTER, REV. JOSEPH V., A.B., J.C.D., Force and Fear as Precluding Matrimonial Consent, V-211 pp., 1932.
81. JAEGER, REV. LEO A., A.B., J.C.D., The Administration of Vacant and Quasi-Vacant Episcopal Sees in the United States, IX-229 pp., 1932.
82. RIMLINGER, REV. HERBERT T., J.C.D., Error Invalidating Matrimonial Consent, VII-79 pp., 1932.
83. BARRETT, REV. JOHN D. M., S.S., J.C.D., A Comparative Study of the Third Plenary Council of Baltimore and the Code, IX-221 pp., 1932.
84. CARBERRY, REV. JOHN J., PH.D., S.T.D., J.C.D., The Juridical Form of Marriage, X-177 pp., 1934.
85. DOLAN, REV. JOHN L., A.B., J.C.D., The Defensor Vinculi, XII-157 pp., 1934.

86. Hannan, Rev. Jerome D., A.M., S.T.D., LL.B., J.C.D., The Canon Law of Wills, IX-517 pp., 1934.
87. Lemieux, Rev. Delise A., A.M., J.C.D., The Sentence in Ecclesiastical Procedure, IX-131 pp., 1934.
88. O'Rourke, Rev. James J., A.B., J.C.D., Parish Registers, VII-109 pp., 1934.
89. Timlin, Rev. Bartholomew, O.F.M., A.M., J.C.D., Conditional Matrimonial Consent, X-381 pp., 1934.
90. Wahl, Rev. Francis X., A.B., J.C.D., The Matrimonial Impediments of Consanguinity and Affinity, VI-125 pp., 1934.
91. White, Rev. Robert J., A.B., LL.B., S.T.B., J.C.D., Canonical Ante-Nuptial Promises and the Civil Law, VI-152 pp., 1934.
92. Herrera, Rev. Antonio Parra, O.C.D., J.C.D., Legislacion Ecclesiastica sobra el Ayuno y la Abstinencia, XI-191 pp., 1935.
93. Kennedy, Rev. Edwin J., J.C.D., The Special Matrimonial Process in Cases of Evident Nullity, X-165 pp., 1935.
94. Manning, Rev. John J., A.B., J.C.D., Presumption of Law in Matrimonial Procedure, XI-111 pp., 1935.
95. Moeder, Rev. John M., J.C.D., The Proper Bishop for Ordination and Dimissorial Letters, VII-135 pp., 1935.
96. O'Mara, Rev. William A., A.B., J.C.D., Canonical Causes for Matrimonial Dispensations, IX-155 pp., 1935.
97. Reilly, Rev. Peter, J.C.D., Residence of Pastors, IX-81 pp., 1935.
98. Smith, Rev. Mariner T., O.P., S.T.Lr., J.C.D., The Penal Law for Religious, VII-169 pp., 1935.
99. Whalen, Rev. Donald W., A.M., J.C.D., The Value of Testimonial Evidence in Matrimonial Procedure, XIII-297 pp., 1935.
100. Cleary, Rev. Joseph F., J.C.D., Canonical Limitations on the Alienation of Church Property, VIII-141 pp., 1936.
101. Glynn, Rev. John C., J.C.D., The Promoter of Justice, XX-337 pp., 1936.
102. Brennan, Rev. James H., S.S., M.A., S.T.B., J.C.D., The Simple Convalidation of Marriage, VI-135 pp., 1937.
103. Bbunini, Rev. Joseph Bernard, J.C.D., The Clerical Obligations of Canons 139 and 142, X-121 pp., 1937.
104. Connor, Rev. Maurice, A.B., J.C.D., The Administrative Removal of Pastors, VIII-159 pp., 1937.
105. Guilfoyle, Rev. Merlin Joseph, J.C.D., Custom, XI-144 pp., 1937.
106. Hughes, Rev. James Austin, A.B., A.M., J.C.D., Witnesses in Criminal Trials of Clerics, IX-140 pp., 1937.
107. Jansen, Rev. Raymond J., A.B., S.T.L., J.C.D., Canonical Provisions for Catechetical Instruction, VII-153 pp., 1937.
108. Kealy, Rev. John James, A.B., J.C.D., The Introductory Libellus in Church Court Procedure, XI-121 pp., 1937.
109. McManus, Rev. James Edward, C.SS.R., J.C.D., The Administration of Temporal Goods in Religious Institutes, XVI-196 pp., 1937.

110. Moriarty, Rev. Eugene James, J.C.D., Oaths in Ecclesiastical Courts, X-115 pp., 1937.
111. Rainer, Rev. Eligius George, C.SS.R., J.C.D., Suspension of Clerics, XVII-249 pp., 1937.
112. Reilly, Rev. Thomas F., C.SS.R., J.C.D., Visitation of Religious, VI-195 pp., 1938.
113. Moriarity, Rev. Francis E., C.SS.R., J.C.D., The Extraordinary Absolution from Censures, XV-334 pp., 1938.
114. Connolly, Rev. Nicholas P., J.C.D., The Canonical Erection of Parishes, X-132 pp., 1938.
115. Donovan, Rev. James Joseph, J.C.D., The Pastor's Obligation in Prenuptial Investigation, XII-322 pp., 1938.
116. Harrigan, Rev. Robert J., M.A., S.T.B., J.C.D., The Radical Sanation of Invalid Marriages, VIII-208 pp., 1938.
117. Boffa, Rev. Conrad Humbert, J.C.D., Canonical Provisions for Catholic Schools, VII-211 pp., 1939.
118. Parsons, Rev. Anscar John, O.M.Cap., J.C.D., Canonical Elections, XII-236 pp., 1939.
119. Reilly, Rev. Edward Michael, A.B., J.C.D., The General Norms of Dispensation, XII-156 pp., 1939.
120. Ryan, Rev. Gerald Aloysius, A.B., J.C.D., Principles of Episcopal Jurisdiction, XII-172 pp., 1939.
121. Burton, Rev. Francis James, C.S.C., A.B., J.C.D., A Commentary on Canon 1125, X-222 pp., 1940.
122. Miaskiewicz, Rev. Francis Sigismund, J.C.D., Supplied Jurisdiction According to Canon 209, XII-340 pp., 1940.
123. Rice, Rev. Patrick William, A.B., J.C.D., Proof of Death in Prenuptial Investigation, VIII-156 pp., 1940.
124. Anglin, Rev. Thomas Francis, M.S., J.C.D., The Eucharistic Fast, VIII-183 pp., 1941.
125. Coleman, Rev. John Jerome, J.C.D., The Minister of Confirmation, VI-153 pp., 1941.
126. Downs, Rev. Joseph Emmanuel, A.B., J.C.D., The Concept of Clerical Immunity, XI-163 pp., 1941.
127. Esswein, Rev. Anthony Albert, J.C.D., Extrajudicial Penal Powers of Ecclesiastical Superiors, X-144 pp., 1941.
128. Farrell, Rev. Benjamin Francis, M.A., S.T.L., J.C.D., The Rights and Duties of the Local Ordinary Regarding Congregations of Women Religious of Pontifical Approval, V-195 pp., 1941.
129. Feeney, Rev. Thomas John, A.B., S.T.L., J.C.D., Restitutio in Integrum, VI-169 pp., 1941.
130. Findlay, Rev. Stephen William, O.S.B., A.B., J.C.D., Canonical Norms Governing the Deposition and Degradation of Clerics, XVII-279 pp., 1941.
131. Goodwine, Rev. John, A.B., S.T.L., J.C.D., The Right of the Church to Acquire Property, VIII-119 pp., 1941.

132. Heston, Rev. Edward Louis, C.S.C., Ph.D., S.T.D., J.C.D., The Alienation of Church Property in the United States, XII-222 pp., 1941.
133. Hogan, Rev. James John, A.B., S.T.L., J.C.D., Judicial Advocates and Procurators, XIII-200 pp., 1941.
134. Kealy, Rev. Thomas M., A.B., Litt.D., J.C.D., Dowry of Women Religious, IX-152 pp., 1941.
135. Keene, Rev. Michael James, O.S.B., J.C.D., Religious Ordinaries and Canon 198, V-164 pp., 1942.
136. Kerin, Rev. Charles A., S.S., M.A., S.T.B., J.C.D., The Privation of Christian Burial, XVI-279 pp., 1941.
137. Louis, Rev. William Francis, M.A., J.C.D., Diocesan Archives, X-101 pp., 1941.
138. McDevitt, Rev. Gilbert Joseph, A.B., J.C.D., Legitimacy and Legitimation, X-247 pp., 1941.
139. McDonough, Rev. Thomas Joseph, A.B., J.C.D., Apostolic Administrators, X-217 pp., 1941.
140. Meier, Rev. Carl Anthony, A.B., J.C.D., Penal Administration Procedure Against Negligent Pastors, XI-240 pp., 1941.
141. Schmidt, Rev. John Rogg, A.B., J.C.D., The Principles of Authentic Interpretation in Canon 17 of the Code of Canon Law, XII-331 pp., 1941.
142. Slafkosky, Rev. Andrew Leonard, A.B., J.C.D., The Canonical Episcopal Visitation of the Diocese, X-197 pp., 1941.
143. Swoboda, Rev. Innocent Robert, O.F.M., J.C.D., Ignorance in Relation to the Imputability of Delicts, IX-271 pp., 1941.
144. Dubé, Rev. Arthur Joseph, A.B., J.C.D., The General Principles for the Reckoning of Time in Canon Law, VIII-299 pp., 1941.
145. McBride, Rev. James T., A.B., J.C.D., Incardination and Excardination of Seculars, XX-585 pp., 1941.
146. Krol, Rev. John T., J.C.D., The Defendant in Ecclesiastical Trials, XII-207 pp., 1942.
147. Comyns, Rev. Joseph J., C.SS.R., A.B., J.C.D., Papal and Episcopal Administration of Church Property, XIV-155 pp., 1942.
148. Barry, Rev. Garrett Francis, O.M.I., J.C.D., Violation of the Cloister, XII-260 pp., 1942.
149. Bolduc, Rev. Gatien, C.S.V., A.B., S.T.L., J.C.D., Les Études dans les Religions Cléricales, VIII-155 pp., 1942.
150. Boyle, Rev. David John, M.A., J.C.D., The Juridic Effects of Moral Certitude on Pre-Nuptial Guarantees, XII-188 pp., 1942.
151. Canavan, Rev. Walter Joseph, M.A., Litt.D., J.C.D., The Profession of Faith, XII-143 pp., 1942.
152. Desrochers, Rev. Bruno, A.B., Ph.L., S.T.B., J.C.D., Le Premier Concile Plénier de Québec et le Code de Droit Canonique, XIV-186 pp., 1942.

153. DILLON, REV. ROBERT EDWARD, A.B., J.C.D., Common Law Marriage, X-148 pp., 1942.
154. DODWELL, REV. EDWARD JOHN, PH.D., S.T.B., J.C.D., The Time and Place for the Celebration of Marriage, X-156 pp., 1942.
155. DONNELLAN, REV. THOMAS ANDREW, A.B., J.C.D., The Obligation of the Misa pro Populo, VII-131 pp., 1942.
156. ELTZ, REV. LOUIS ANTHONY, A.B., J.C.L., Cooperation in Crime.
157. GASS, REV. SYLVESTER FRANCIS, M.A., J.C.D., Ecclesiastical Pensions, XI-206 pp., 1942.
158. GUINIVEN, REV. JOHN JOSEPH, C.SS.R., J.C.D., The Precept of Hearing Mass, XIV-188 pp., 1942.
159. GULCZYNSKI, REV. JOHN THEOPHILUS, J.C.D., The Desecration and Violation of Churches, X-126 pp., 1942.
160. HAMMILL, REV. JOHN LEO, M.A., J.C.D., The Obligations of the Traveler According to Canon 14, VIII-204 pp., 1942.
161. HAYDT, REV. JOHN JOSEPH, A.B., J.C.D., Reserved Benefices, XI-148 pp., 1942.
162. HUSER, REV. ROGER JOHN, O.F.M., A.B., J.C.D., The Crime of Abortion in Canon Law, XII-187 pp., 1942.
163. KEARNEY, REV. FRANCIS PATRICK, A.B., S.T.L., J.C.L., The Principles of Canon 1127
164. LINAHEN, REV. LEO JAMES, S.T.L., J.C.D., De Absolutione Complicis In Peccato Turpi, 114 pp., 1942.
165. MCCLOSKEY, REV. JOSEPH ALOYSIUS, A.B., J.C.D., The Subject of Ecclesiastical Law According to Canon 12, XVII-246 pp., 1942.
166. O'NEILL, REV. FRANCIS JOSEPH, C.SS.R., J.C.D., The Dismissal of Religious in Temporary Vows, XIII-220 pp., 1942.
167. PRINCE, REV. JOHN EDWARD, A.B., S.T.D., J.C.D., The Diocesan Chancellor, X-136 pp., 1942.
168. RIESNER, REV. ALBERT JOSEPH, C.SS.R., J.C.D., Apostates and Fugitives from Religious Institutes, IX-168 pp., 1942.
169. STENGER, REV. JOSEPH BERNARD, J.C.D., The Mortgaging of Church Property, 186 pp., 1942.
170. WALDRON, REV. JOSEPH FRANCIS, A.B., J.C.D., The Minister of Baptism, XII-197 pp., 1942.
171. WILLETT, REV. ROBERT ALBERT, J.C.D., The Probative Value of Documents in Ecclesiastical Trials, X-124 pp., 1942.
172. WOEBER, REV. EDWARD MARTIN, M.A., J.C.D., The Interpellations, XII-161 pp., 1942.
173. BENKO, REV. MATTHEW ALOYSIUS, O.S.B., M.A., J.C.L., The Abbot *Nullius*.
174. CHRIST, REV. JOSEPH JAMES, M.A., S.T.L., J.C.L., Dispensation from Vindicative Penalties.
175. CLANCY, REV. PATRICK M. J., O.P., A.B., S.T.LR., J.C.D., The Local Religious Superior, X-299 pp., 1943.

176. Clarke, Rev. Thomas James, J.C.D., Parish Societies, XII-147 pp., 1943.
177. Connolly, Rev. John Patrick, S.T.L., J.C.D., Synodal Examiners and Parish Priest Consultors, X-223 pp., 1943.
178. Drumm, Rev. William Martin, A.B., J.C.L., Hospital Chaplains.
179. Flanagan, Rev. Bernard Joseph, A.B., S.T.L., J.C.D., The Canonical Erection of Religious Houses, X-147 pp., 1943.
180. Kelleher, Rev. Stephen Joseph, A.B., S.T.B., J.C.D., Discussions with non-Catholics: Canonical Legislation, X-93 pp., 1943.
181. Lewis, Rev. Gordian, C.P., J.C.D., Chapters in Religious Institutes, XII-169 pp., 1943.
182. Marx, Rev. Adolph, J.C.D., The Declaration of Nullity of Marriages Contracted Outside the Church, X-151 pp., 1943.
183. Matulenas, Rev. Raymond Anthony, O.S.B., A.B., J.C.L., Communication, a Source of Privileges.
184. O'Leary, Rev. Charles Gerard, C.SS.R., J.C.D., Religious Dismissed After Perpetual Profession, X-213 pp., 1943.
185. Power, Rev. Cornelius Michael, J.C.L., The Blessing of Cemeteries.
186. Shuhler, Rev. Ralph Vincent, O.S.A., J.C.D., Privileges of Regulars to Absolve and Dispense, XII-195 pp., 1943.
187. Ziolkowski, Rev. Thaddeus Stanislaus, A.B., J.C.D., The Consecration and Blessing of Churches, XII-151 pp., 1943.
188. Heneghan, Rev. John Joseph, S.T.D., J.C.L., The Marriages of Unworthy Catholics: Canons 1065 and 1066.
189. Carroll, Rev. Coleman Francis, M.A., S.T.L., J.C.L., Charitable Institutions.
190. Ciesluk, Rev. Joseph Edward, Ph.B., S.T.L., J.C.L., National Parishes in the United States.
191. Coburn, Rev. Vincent Paul, A.B., J.C.L., Marriages of Conscience.
192. Connors, Rev. Charles Paul, C.S.Sp., A.B., J.C.L., Extra-Judicial Procurators in the Code of Canon Law.
193. Coyle, Rev. Paul Raymond, A.B., J.C.L., Judicial Exceptions.
194. Fair, Rev. Bartholomew Francis, A.B., S.T.L., J.C.L., The Impediment of Abduction.
195. Gallagher, Rev. Thomas Raphael, O.P., A.B., S.T.Lr., J.C.L., The Examination of the Qualities of the Ordinand.
196. Gannon, Rev. John Mark, S.T.L., J.C.L., The Interstices Required for the Promotion to Orders.
197. Goldsmith, Rev. J. William, B.C.S., S.T.L., J.C.L., The Competence of Church and State over Marriage—Disputed Points.
198. Goodwine, Rev. Joseph Gerard, A.B., S.T.B., J.C.L., The Reception of Converts.
199. Kowalski, Rev. Romuald Eugene, O.F.M., A.B., J.C.L., Sustenance of Religious Houses of Regulars.
200. McCoy, Rev. Alan Edward, O.F.M., J.C.L., Force and Fear in Relation to Delictual Imputability and Penal Responsibility.

201. McDevitt, Rev. Vincent John, Ph.B., S.T.L., J.C.L., Perjury.
202. Martin, Rev. Thomas Owen, Ph.D., S.T.D., J.C.L., Adverse Possession, Prescription and Limitation of Actions: The Canonical "Praescriptio."
203. Miklosovic, Rev. Paul John, A.B., J.C.L., Attempted Marriages and Their Consequent Juridic Effects.
204. Mundy, Rev. Thomas Maurice, A.B., S.T.L., J.C.L., The Union of Parishes.
205. O'Dea, Rev. John Coyle, A.B., J.C.L., The Matrimonial Impediment of Nonage.
206. Olalia, Rev. Alexander Ayson, S.T.L., J.C.L., A Comparative Study of the Christian Constitution of States and the Constitution of the Philippine Commonwealth.
207. Poisson, Rev. Pierre-Marie, C.S.C., A.B., Ph.L., Th.L., J.C.L., Droits Patrimoniaux des Maisons et des Eglises Religieuses.
208. Stadalnikas, Rev. Casimir Joseph, M.I.C., J.C.L., Reservation of Censures.
209. Sullivan, Rev. Eugene Henry, S.T.L., J.C.L., Proof of the Reception of the Sacraments.
210. Vaughan, Rev. William Edward, J.C.L., Constitutions for Diocesan Courts.
211. Lyons, Rev. Joseph Henry, J.C.L., The Joinder of Issue in Canonical Trials.

INDEX

www.ingramcontent.com/pod-product-compliance
Lightning Source LLC
LaVergne TN
LVHW050211080826
844660LV00012B/398
* 9 7 8 0 8 1 3 2 2 3 9 1 9 *